ISO 26000

The Business Guide to the new Standard on Social Responsibility

ISO 26000
THE BUSINESS GUIDE
to the new
Standard on Social Responsibility

Lars Moratis and Timo Cochius

Routledge
Taylor & Francis Group

LONDON AND NEW YORK

First published 2011 by Greenleaf Publishing Limited

Published 2017 by Routledge
2 Park Square, Milton Park, Abingdon, Oxon OX14 4RN
711 Third Avenue, New York, NY 10017, USA

Routledge is an imprint of the Taylor & Francis Group, an informa business

Cover by LaliAbril.com

British Library Cataloguing in Publication Data:
    Moratis, L. T. (Lars T.)
        The business guide to the new standard on social
        responsibility. -- (ISO 26000 ; v. 1)
        1. Social responsibility of business--Standards. 2. Social
        responsibility of business.
        I. Title II. Series III. Cochius, Timo. IV. International
        Organization for Standardization.
        658.4'08'0218-dc22

        ISBN-13: 9781906093402 (pbk)

Contents

Preface vii

1 Introduction 1

2 What is social responsibility (according to ISO 26000)? 9

Interlude I: SR in practice: motivations, manifestations and results 27

3 ISO 26000: background, characteristics and structure 33

Interlude II: Myths and misunderstandings about ISO 26000: Part 1 59

4 SR principles 65

Interlude III: Myths and misunderstandings about ISO 26000: Part 2 79

5 Stakeholder identification and engagement 83

Interlude IV: Frequently asked questions about ISO 26000 101

6 SR core subjects and issues 107

Interlude V: The materiality of ISO 26000 for SMEs 141

7 Selecting SR priorities 145

8 SR implementation 163

9 Epilogue: final thoughts on (the future of) ISO 26000 179

Bibliography 187

Annex 1: ISO 26000 Quick Scan 190

Annex 2: An exercise to identify stakeholders' interests
and expectations 195

Annex 3: The SR performance form 198

Annex 4: Millennium Development Goals. 201

Annex 5: The Global Compact 203

About the authors 206

Preface

As CSR experts, we are confronted with questions from various types of organisations about how they can build authentic CSR policies and implement these successfully. The essence of their questions is threefold: what are the responsibilities of their organisation; how can they create value with CSR; and how can they implement CSR? Those three questions capture the core of the profession of a CSR consultant. Only when an organisation is aware of its societal impacts (what we will refer to in this book as its social and environmental footprints), has a true and deep concern for these impacts, and consciously acts according to this concern at both a strategic and operational level, can one speak of an integration of the 3Ps of people, planet and profit, or the triple bottom line as coined by John Elkington in the mid-1990s. That is what it is all about—and that is the big challenge.

Over the years, we have developed an approach to effectively deal with this challenge. One of the central starting points of our approach is that every organisation has its own individual, organisation-specific CSR profile. In other words: every organisation should interpret CSR in a way that fits its activities, impacts and sphere of influence. We call this CSR 2.0 (see Chapter 3). CSR should have an organisation-specific meaning. For some, this may seem a 'soft' approach or notion, but we believe the contrary to be the case: this is a very business-oriented way to approach CSR that leads to multiple benefits—profits for the organisation and profits (prosperity) for society. By following this approach, CSR gets aligned with the *raison d'être* of the organisation—its reasons for operating, its ambitions and goals, the markets or target groups it serves, the way the organisation tries to accomplish its goals and reach its target groups, the products and services it produces and what's important to the people within the organisation. That simple notion—alignment—is one of the most important ingredients for effective implementation.

ISO 26000, the new global guidance document for SR (social responsibility)[1] published in November 2010, *can* become an important instrument for designing the CSR implementation process. We stress the word *can*, as at the time of writing there is no evidence to sufficiently support a bolder claim. Still, we expect that ISO 26000, with all its advantages, disadvantages, possibilities and difficulties, will become an authoritative guideline for (the implementation of) SR. At the same time, a lot of questions are arising and various misunderstandings have surfaced about this new guidance. We think that ISO 26000 is extremely important and deserves attention. It also deserves explanation, and that is one of the main reasons for writing this book.

As well as looking at the background, content and principles of ISO 26000, we have also seized the opportunity to expound our own interpretations, ideas and experiences of SR. In this book, we've written down what in our opinion are the basic notions behind the SR concept, its fundamental tenets and the implementation challenges it brings. Also, we have included many illustrations and examples of SR as it manifests and can manifest itself in practice. In essence, we think that ISO 26000 can be a highly useful guide in determining an organisation's social responsibilities and helping it to implement a proper SR strategy.

We have benefited greatly from discussions with colleagues, clients and various CSR professionals in developing this book. All these people have inspired us in one way or the other and we owe them a huge thank-you. We particularly thank Sanne Hoefnagels for her support and John Stuart at Greenleaf Publishing for giving us the opportunity to publish this book. To Inge, Elsa and Suzan: thank you for your own, unique contributions to this project. Also, we thank John Stuart and Dean Bargh at Greenleaf Publishing for entering into this project with us, their patience and their useful help in the process of finishing this book. We would also like to acknowledge the efforts made by the experts, enthusiasts and organisations that contributed to the development of ISO 26000 over the years. They have done an excellent job in reconciling different views and interests and arriving at a universal guidance document. Finally, we must thank Jon Kirke at the BSI (British Standards Institution) for granting

---

1 The distinction between 'CSR' and 'SR' is rather trivial, in our opinion. The main purpose in ISO 26000 of labelling the concept of 'CSR' as 'SR' has been to imply that ISO 26000 applies not only to companies, but in fact to any type of organisation, irrespective of its activities and size. From here on, and in line with ISO 26000, we will use the term 'SR' in preference to 'CSR'.

permission for us to reproduce extracts from ISO 26000.[2] We should also say here that in order to get the maximum benefit from this book, obtaining a copy of ISO 26000 from ISO or a national standards body is highly recommended.

Besides giving our thanks we hope that by publishing this book we do justice to all of these people, their efforts and their ideas. What we have in common is an ambition to enable organisations to play an increasingly larger role in sustainable development in ways that fit and benefit their organisations and the societies in which they operate.

We hope that the same is the case for the role this book may play in the CSR ambitions of others—of people and organisations that we don't know (yet) and with whom we could maybe work with in the future. Hopefully, they will also find this book valuable and it will be a meaningful contribution to their CSR quest.

Lars Moratis
Timo Cochius
Rotterdam, March 2011

---

2 All extracts from ISO 26000 included in this book have been granted by BSI on behalf of ISO. ISO standards can be obtained in PDF or hard-copy formats from the ISO online shop: www.iso.org/iso/store.htm.

1

Introduction

1.1 **An emerging morality: the new business doctrine**

Interest in CSR (corporate social responsibility) is increasing daily. As one of the most visible management themes of the 21st century it has captured the attention of many organisations around the world—and not just businesses, but also governments and NGOs (non-governmental organisations). CSR has become part of many marketing campaigns, a key criterion in procurement, an instrument for recruiting and retaining talented employees, a source of innovation, an entrepreneurial opportunity, a profit-driver and even an export product, to use the words of the Dutch Secretary of Economic Affairs of the Balkenende IV administration, Frank Heemskerk (Volkskrant 2007).

At the same time, CSR is a reflection of an emerging new organisational morality, a way to express values and identities, perhaps as an acknowledgement of something that many organisations already 'do'—simply because they think it important. CSR also has great societal relevance, since businesses, governments and NGOs have a central role in contributing to what might be the most important challenge of our times: realising sustainable development. This emerging morality is illustrated in the new global guidance document ISO 26000.[1]

---

1 'Social responsibility has the organisation as its focus and concerns the responsibilities of an organisation to society and the environment. Social responsibility is closely linked to sustainable development. Because sustainable development is

CSR has also obtained a role in the development and education of new generations of managers, directors, administrators and entrepreneurs. The subject is constantly evolving and may now be described as both a management philosophy and a modern economic doctrine. The American business scholar Dow Votaw wrote as long ago as 1972 that corporate social responsibility means something, but not always the same thing to everybody (Votaw 1972). CSR, it sometimes seems, is everything and everywhere.

Within this jungle of CSR themes, initiatives and views, many organisations are urgently in need of an overview, structure and roadmap on how to engage with CSR in practice. What does CSR mean to them? For many organisations, engagement would be far easier if there were a way to design a CSR policy to fit with their own uniqueness and characteristics, including the context in which they operate. Many organisations are also in need of guidance and advice in the field of *implementing* CSR—creating enthusiasm and buy-in both internally and externally, and practising CSR on a day-to-day basis.

1.1.2 A note on terminologies

ISO 26000, the new global guidance document for SR (social responsibility) has been developed to address these problems. But, before we look at ISO 26000 in more detail, there's a terminology thing to settle: SR or CSR? ISO took the decision that its guidance should be appropriate for *all* organisations: not just big business (as the 'C' in CSR implies), but governments, NGOs and businesses of all sizes. This is an important distinction. Therefore, although it is our intention in this book to primarily explain the standard in terms of its potential usage by business (and 'CSR' has clearly been the term in common use thus far) we will follow the lead set by ISO 26000 and generally use the term 'SR' unless we are talking specifically about corporations or known CSR initiatives.

---

about the economic, social and environmental goals common to all people, it can be used as a way of summing up the broader expectations of society that need to be taken into account by organisations seeking to act responsibly. Therefore, an overarching objective of an organisation's social responsibility should be to contribute to sustainable development' (ISO 2010: 9).

1.2 **Creating clarity and uniformity**

ISO's ambition was to develop a global and overarching guidance document which could create clarity and uniformity in SR concepts, define essential SR topics, provide advice about the ways in which organisations can identify their social responsibilities and show how SR can be integrated not only into companies, but into all types of organisations. A vast array of stakeholder groups have been involved in the process. ISO 26000 is also a new branch on the thriving tree of SR standards, of which more and more have emerged over the past few years—some in the field of CSR sub-areas, such as Account-Ability's AA1000 series on stakeholder engagement, with others focusing on CSR as a whole, such as the Global Reporting Initiative (GRI) guidelines on sustainability reporting. Still, ISO 26000 is rather different to these initiatives and is likely to become the single most significant development in the field for years to come. For tens of thousands of organisations around the world ISO 26000 may well provide the foundation for their SR policies.

1.2.1 Why this book—and why now?

The finalisation of ISO 26000 and its release in November 2010 means that the guidance it provides needs explanation for potential business users. Research conducted in 2009 by Brandsma *et al.* among 221 Dutch organisations (both SMEs and large companies) showed that more than half of the respondents (54%) were only in the initial stages of implementing policies on SR. Almost 15% of organisations indicated that they had not taken any steps at all. The results also highlighted the clear lack of knowledge, a plan or strategies to implement SR (see Fig. 1.1). ISO 26000—and this book—may come at the right time for such organisations.

Despite its short history, a number of myths and misunderstandings regarding ISO 26000 have already surfaced. There appears to be confusion among many potential users about the scope and status of the guidance, its applicability to different kinds of organisations, its relationship with other standards (for example, in the fields of quality, environment, safety, health and information security) and, crucially, whether it will be possible to certify against it. Clearly, such confusion neither promotes the usage of ISO 26000 nor the implementation of SR in general. This book attempts to clarify these myths and misunderstandings by describing and analysing what ISO 26000 is—and what it isn't.

The intention of this book is to examine the content and the ideas behind ISO 26000 in a clear and understandable way. Both organisations that want

Figure 1.1 **Barriers for CSR implementation**

Source: Brandsma *et al.* 2009

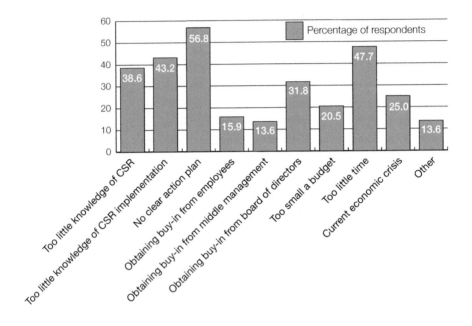

to learn more about the 'why, what and how' of ISO 26000 and those that are interested in basing their SR policy on it (or who want to organise existing policies in accordance with the new standard) can benefit from this book. It is not our intention to elaborate on all of the subjects dealt with in ISO 26000 in great detail. That would be an impossible task—many of these subjects warrant (and in many cases already have) separate books all to themselves. There are literally hundreds of tools dealing with individual SR subjects and the themes that are included within ISO 26000. The fact that these materials have not yet found their way into many organisations around the world is another issue entirely.

Despite the fact that the text of ISO 26000 is the starting point of this book, we also provide relevant background material regarding the development of the guidance, real-life examples, reflections and several practical tools (such as an ISO 26000 quick scan and a method for identifying stakeholders), as well as experiential implementation tips that can be used in practice by different organisations.

1.3 **Outline of this book**

This book contains nine chapters, six interludes and five annexes. After having read the chapters the reader should have developed a clear understanding of SR and ISO 26000. The book is full of real-life examples, 'did-you-know' boxes and illustrative material.

This book largely follows the overall structure of ISO 26000. Hence, the core of the book consists of the four main clauses of ISO 26000:

- SR principles (Clause 4)

- The identification of stakeholders and the creation of stakeholder engagement (Clause 5)

- The core subjects and issues of SR (Clause 6)

- The integration of SR throughout the organisation (Clause 7)

Clause 4 and Clause 6 essentially deal with 'the contents of SR' (SR-related starting points and themes); Clause 5 and Clause 7 essentially deal with 'the process of SR' (implementing and integrating SR into an organisation). We do diverge slightly from the standard's structure. For example, Clause 7 has been divided into two parts in this book: the selection of SR priorities; and the SR implementation process.

Did you know...

The PricewaterhouseCoopers Sustainability Barometer of September 2009 showed that only 40% of Dutch companies have linked business goals to their CSR strategies.

1.3.1 Chapter outline

After this introduction, we briefly introduce SR (Chapter 2). The meaning of the term and its origin are explored and several generally accepted views, interpretations and characteristics are discussed. Chapter 2 also considers a number of the SR core subjects included in ISO 26000, both from a conceptual and a practical angle, and explores the concept of SR as it is defined in ISO 26000. One key theme here is the emphasis the guidance gives to *morality* as a driver for SR. Much of the discourse in the business world regarding CSR has been around the *business case*. Perhaps because the intention of ISO 26000 is to be relevant to *all* organisations, we hear little of the business reasons for action.

We follow Chapter 2 with the first of six interludes. These are inserted throughout the book as additional short explanations or illustrations of the practice of SR and ISO 26000. Interlude I examines motives for, manifestations of and outcomes of SR in practice.

Chapter 3 discusses ISO 26000 more specifically and starts with characterising where the guidance fits within the burgeoning field of CSR-related codes, guidelines, norms and standards. We look at the reasons behind its development, its ambition, scope, objectives and functions. We also examine the new concept of the SR profile introduced in ISO 26000. This approach provides room for a definition of SR that fits the uniqueness of different organisations. This organisation-specific definition of SR is a characteristic of a new generation of SR, which we label 'SR 2.0' and consequently elaborate on. Chapter 3 concludes by summarising the layout and content of ISO 26000. The structure of ISO 26000 is briefly discussed and its clauses are explained. Here, attention is also paid to the way in which the actions and expectations of organisations are defined within ISO 26000.

In the second interlude, we attempt to clarify the first three of a total of six myths and misunderstandings that exist about ISO 26000.

Chapter 4 deals with the first of the four core clauses of ISO 26000: the SR principles. Here, the general SR principles (which have to be distinguished from the principles specified for each of the core subjects in ISO 26000) are discussed. These principles form the pillars of ISO 26000 and are related to all other parts of the guidance. This chapter begins by stressing the importance and the role of principles and their application within (C)SR. Consequently, the general SR principles are described. We also look at other potential principles, not included in ISO 26000 but which perhaps could and should have been. Finally, the chapter considers the expectations ISO 26000 spells out for organisations in dealing with these principles.

Interlude III examines the final three myths and misunderstandings about ISO 26000.

Chapter 5 concerns perhaps the most prominent SR principle within ISO 26000—respect for stakeholder interests. We therefore consider the identification of stakeholders and their interests, and the management of stakeholder engagement. This principle, and hence this chapter, deals with the relationships between the organisation, its stakeholders and society as a whole. We discuss how organisations can identify their stakeholders and their interests, illustrated with several examples. Subsequently, we examine the reasons for creating stakeholder engagement programmes, actions that an organisation should undertake in this area and ways to involve stakeholders in the SR policy of an organisation.

The fourth interlude contains a number of frequently asked questions about ISO 26000—and the answers to these questions.

The SR core subjects and issues that ISO 26000 specifies are described in Chapter 6. We discuss practicalities and potential problems for organisations. After an initial overview of the core subjects and issues, their structure within ISO 26000 is explained. Furthermore, this chapter provides numerous examples of the (often brief) descriptions, related principles and starting points from which the SR core subjects have developed. However, the meat of this chapter concentrates on the expectations that ISO 26000 has for organisations that want to base their SR policy on the guideline. All of the SR issues are illustrated with real-life examples to illustrate ISO 26000's potential application.

The next interlude focuses on the materiality (relevance) of the SR principles, SR core subjects and SR issues for SMEs (small and medium-sized enterprises). This was the subject of a study conducted by the IISD (International Institute for Sustainable Development) at the end of 2008 (Perera 2008). The results of this research offered interesting insights into how both potential users and certain experts perceive the relevance of ISO 26000 for SMEs.

Chapter 7 covers the first part of Clause 7 of ISO 26000, and addresses how organisations should select SR priorities. In line with the idea of an organisation-specific SR profile, ISO 26000 asks the user to define the main areas that they want to focus their SR policy on. ISO 26000 encourages organisations to formulate their own SR priorities, based on the idea of their sustainability impact (the effects an organisation has on people, environment, stakeholders and society). How an organisation defines the 'relevance' and 'significance' of SR core subjects and related issues, as well as the sphere of influence an organisation has, play a central role in this chapter. The chapter ends with advice on the selection of SR priorities.

Chapter 8 concentrates on the second part of Clause 7: integrating SR into the organisation. It consequently deals with SR implementation—a major challenge for many organisations. Creating support for SR and engaging stakeholders are just two of the common problems experienced. This chapter discusses the considerations and suggestions that ISO 26000 provides on SR implementation. Furthermore, attention is paid to communicating SR (for example, the functions and methods of SR communication), enhancing the credibility of SR initiatives and monitoring and improving SR performance.

The final chapter contains a number of concluding thoughts and remarks about ISO 26000. This epilogue discusses, among other things, possible futures for ISO 26000, such as whether certification or alternatives for certification are likely, the potential contractual use of ISO 26000 and further speculation regarding the further development of ISO 26000 when it is revised in the coming years.

2

What is social responsibility (according to ISO 26000)?

2.1 **Introduction**

A lot of uncertainty exists around the concept of organisational social responsibility. It has been labelled a 'container concept' (Van Weele 2009) which expresses a vague notion about the morality of organisations, but by others it is seen as a corporate strategy that is derived from trends and developments in both markets and society. At the very least, CSR (corporate social responsibility) is a meaningful concept in several respects and it is important to get an understanding of its key concepts and definitions. This chapter provides a brief introduction to the history and background of CSR, and gives several definitions as well as explanations on key aspects of these definitions. The concepts of responsibility and accountability take centre stage in explaining the essence of CSR. Also in this chapter, a clear distinction is made between CSR and corporate community involvement, although the latter can be seen as an integral part of the former.

As noted in Chapter 1 (see §1.1.2), ISO 26000 deliberately uses the term 'social responsibility' rather than the more common 'CSR'. The first half of this chapter deals with the definition and interpretation of CSR while the second half looks at SR as used in ISO 26000.

2.2 **What exactly is CSR?**

The question 'What is CSR?' can be answered in many different ways, both practical and conceptual. The concept's key characteristic is the variety of definitions and opinions it attracts, a feature that is both a strength and a weakness. In the following sections the background to CSR will be discussed and the concept will be dissected into its essence.

2.2.1 A notion with many meanings

More and more topics are being categorised under the banner of CSR, which continues to inflate its meaning. On the other hand, certain themes or behavioural characteristics of organisations are sometimes intentionally kept out of the CSR concept, such as compliance with laws and rules, community involvement or philanthropy. Many synonyms are used to address the same or similar concepts, often with their own nuances, such as social entrepreneurship, sustainable business, value-driven business, ethical business, decent business and corporate citizenship. Add to this the fact that it is sometimes said that doing business is, by definition, socially responsible, and the chaos is complete. Consequently, discussions about CSR are confused by different interpretations. This is increasingly the case because of the ongoing debate about the importance and the meaning of CSR—it is a dynamic not a static concept, and its concerns change in conjunction with developments in markets and society.[1]

The widespread recognition and the legitimacy of the triple-bottom-line concept of the 3Ps (people, planet, profit) resulted in CSR being seen more as a business concept. This concept, introduced by John Elkington in the mid-1990s, argues that paying attention to people (social justice), environment (ecological quality) and society (societal well-being or prosperity) can go hand in hand with creating economic value for organisations. Further, Elkington (1997) argued that only those organisations that systematically align their goals with the goals of society and recognise the interdependence of

---

1 In this debate differences in the national organisational contexts and cultures play a role as well.

the 3Ps will be successful and survive in the future. People, planet and profit *have to* go hand in hand. Many other developments have a role in this, such as the fact that various governments and public sector authorities, including the Dutch, Danish, British and Belgian, increasingly procure sustainably. This way, governments use their influence as a market actor to give a 'sustainability impulse' to the market.

Increasingly, companies are responding to such developments and recognise the market opportunities that CSR brings—not only in their commercial market, but also, for example, in the labour market. Finally, wake-up calls such as the *Stern Review on the Economics of Climate Change* (Stern 2006) and Al Gore's *An Inconvenient Truth*, both from 2006, contributed to the acceptance and uptake of the role of business in combating climate change. Many companies now argue that it is in society's own interest, and thus also in the interest of organisations, to act to mitigate climate change. These sorts of developments contribute to the process of 'societisation' of organisations (Van Dijk 1975): a situation of increasingly radical effects of organisations on society and of increasingly radical demands of society regarding the functioning of organisations.

Did you know…

The Belgian government has adopted a plan for the period 2009–11 aimed at reaching a rate of 50% sustainable procurement in 2011. The Dutch national government already assesses all its procurement against sustainability criteria.

It is obvious that this process of societisation is taking place at a faster and faster rate. CSR has become more visible and important in the past few years for companies, governments and NGOs alike. Not a day goes by without media attention on the urgency of sustainability issues such as the climate crisis, the food crisis, the energy crisis and global poverty—how companies cause and contribute to these crises, what the (possible) consequences are for them and society, and how they can be part of the solution.

The majority of publicly listed companies have developed CSR strategies and report annually on the successes (and sometimes failures) of these strategies—usually in stand-alone sustainability reports and occasionally in their regular annual reports. Principles of corporate governance are increasingly important because of the bankruptcy of a few, now infamous companies, Enron, Parmalat and global investment banks, the economic crisis and society's discontent

Did you know…

Edelman's 2007 Trust Barometer shows that citizens think that businesses can play a vital role in solving environmental problems and social issues that cannot be solved by other parties. In Asia 72% of citizens thought so, in North America 71%, in the EU 57% and in Latin America 63%.

with exorbitant executive pay. Large multinationals such as Philips and Siemens already realise substantial percentages of their revenues through innovative 'green products' and see opportunities to tap new markets with smart approaches such as base-of-the-pyramid strategies[2] which aim to improve the standard of living of people in developing countries. Even within SMEs, CSR has become more commonplace: next to individual companies such as Peeze, Triodos, Gulpener (The Netherlands), Asap Photographic Services (Belgium), Galfinband (Romania), Monnalisa (Italy), Harineras Villamayor (Spain) and Sånga-Säby (Sweden) there are several sectoral organisations, business networks and chambers of commerce active in the field of CSR. Citizens and (future) employees increasingly expect companies to act as 'corporate citizens'. New graduates appear to find attention to CSR by their prospective employers increasingly important. Moreover, the numbers of 'green' consumers, who are inclined to buy sustainable products and services, are growing, as is the market for Fair Trade products.

2.2.2 CSR: nothing new

It is a mistake to think that CSR is a recent phenomenon. The concept is, in fact, anything but new. What is new is the pace with which attention on CSR has been increasing during the past years. In the industrial revolution, many entrepreneurs took good care of their employees by investing in social issues, for instance in the field of housing and education. An important reason for this was to improve employees' health and well-being, and so protect their own interests: in the words of management philosopher Charles Handy, such philanthropic employers showed 'proper selfishness' (Handy 1998).

Discussions and reflections on the social responsibilities of managers and companies go a long way back in time. It could even be argued that the notion of CSR is as old as capitalism itself. A good illustration of this is from one of the founders of capitalism, Adam Smith (most famously known for the idea of 'the invisible hand'). Even though *An Inquiry into the Nature and Causes of the Wealth of Nations* (Smith 1776) is without doubt his most

Did you know...

In 1920, African kings donated money for starving children in Europe.[3]

---

2 These are strategies with which companies offer the poorest people access to products and services that are linked to their needs and possibilities on a commercial basis.

3 M. Ritter, 'The origins of the Bessie Head archive'; www.thuto.org/bhead/html/museum/Origins%20of%20the%20Bessie%20Head%20Archive.pdf, accessed 17 April 2011.

famous work, in 1759 he had already written *The Theory of Moral Sentiments* (Smith 1759) in which he emphasises the importance of ethical forces in the free-market mechanism and international trade, taking into account restrictions from a viewpoint of natural justice to prevent a dominance of amoral egoism. Hence, what Smith wrote in the century before the industrial revolution in *The Wealth of Nations* has to be seen in the context of his previous work.

In the first half of the 20th century *The Functions of the Executive* by Chester Barnard (1938) and *Measurement of Social Performance of Business* by Theodore Kreps (1940) were published, both of which drew attention to the social responsibility of management and companies. Halfway through the 1940s, research conducted by business magazine *Fortune* on corporate managers' ideas about social responsibilities revealed that 93% of the respondents agreed with the hypothesis that they are responsible for the consequences of their decisions other than those visible on the profit and loss account. The early 1950s saw the publication of *Social Responsibilities of the Businessman* by Howard Bowen (1953). This is one of the first important books in the field of CSR and is the starting point of the modern era regarding CSR thinking. The book discussed the observation that the largest companies are important centres of power and decision-making, and that the actions of these companies affect the lives of citizens in several ways. This book notes that change is a dominant feature of life and that this change requires greater recognition and acceptance of social responsibility by business. According to Bowen, CSR is about 'the obligations of businessmen to pursue those policies, to make those decisions, or to follow those lines of action which are desirable in terms of the objectives and values of our society' (Bowen 1953: 6).

Around the same time some other important publications about CSR appeared, such as *Management's Responsibility to Society: The Growth of an Idea* by Morrell Heald (1957) and *Corporate Giving in a Free Society* by Richard Eells (1956). In 1960 Keith Davis described CSR as 'businessmen's decisions and actions taken for reasons at least partially beyond the firm's direct economic or technical interest' (David 1960: 70). In 1963 Joseph W. McGuire wrote in his book *Business and Society* that 'the idea of social responsibilities supposes that the corporation has not only economic and legal obligations but also certain responsibilities to society which extend beyond these obligations' (Maguire 1963: 144). Clarence C. Walton (1967) stated in his book *Corporate Social Responsibilities* that companies should voluntarily acknowledge and accept that they have responsibilities beyond the gates of the company. In 1972, the *Limits to Growth* described the devastating environmental effects of economic growth (Meadows *et al.* 1972). The rest, as they say, is history.

The current interest in CSR also comes from other areas and disciplines. Within the field of quality management, for example, there has been huge attention on the responsibilities, values and ethical behaviour of organisations, witnessed by the visions and opinions of several quality gurus. Crosby (1986; see also McAdam and Leonard 2003: 37) stated that 'the company will prosper only when all employees feel the same way and when neither customers nor employees will be hassled'. Management models such as those of the EFQM framework also give explicit attention to CSR—and this attention is growing. EFQM perceives the social responsibility of organisations as one of the pillars of excellence. In the INK model, a Dutch spin-off of the EFQM framework, extra attention is paid to CSR and sustainability. The explanation for the organisation area 'society' illustrates this: 'Every organisation does not only supply services to (members of) society, but is also part of society. Therefore, it is necessary that the organisation becomes aware of its responsibility for its surroundings: the environment, society and the developments that are taking place'. INK asks organisations what their efforts in the field of social responsibility have yielded. Strategic management and marketing management have, in recent years, shown increasing interest in SR, largely due to its economic value. In 2005, marketing guru Philip Kotler issued *Corporate Social Responsibility: Doing the Most Good for your Company and Your Cause* (Kotler and Lee 2005) and, in 2006, the now well-known article 'Strategy and Society: The Link between Competitive Advantage And Corporate Social Responsibility' was published (Porter and Kramer 2006). Strategy guru C.K. Prahalad has developed the strategy concept 'the bottom of the pyramid' (Prahalad 2004) aimed at doing business with the poor and Peter Drucker, guru of all management gurus, has discussed CSR-related issues during a large part of his career (e.g. Drucker 1999).

Did you know...

An EIM Business & Policy Research (Hoevenagel 2004) study showed that 68% of SME entrepreneurs in the Netherlands know about the concept of CSR. Just 34% of respondents indicated that they were pursuing CSR activities, but when given examples of typical activities, 61% agreed that they actually were pursuing one or more of these.

2.2.3 A few accepted definitions

So what *is* CSR essentially about? According to Nobel Prize-winning economist Milton Friedman it is actually pretty simple. In his view, there is one and only one social responsibility of business—to use its resources and engage in activities designed to increase its profits so long as it stays within the rules of the game, which is to say, engages in open and free competition without deception or fraud (Friedman 1970).

One of Friedman's most oft-cited statements is that 'the business of business is business'. Companies are supposed to take care of the financial interests of shareholders—nothing more and nothing less. Every bit of attention or money spent by management on other business aims is in contradiction to Friedman's law. So Friedman would argue that most CSR activities have no legitimacy and that companies should refrain from getting involved. Only when CSR contributes to the financial performance of a company would the board be allowed to allocate resources to it. In other words: CSR is allowed, but *only* when there is a business—rather than a moral—case for it.

Even though Friedman's view is the radical view of an economist who was a strict supporter of the classical school, his opinion is still shared by many others these days, such as Karnani (2010). One of the most powerful counter-definitions of CSR comes from Archie Carroll (1979). According to Carroll, CSR has an economic, legal, ethical and philanthropic face. This means that companies have the responsibility to be profitable by producing desired goods and services, by obeying laws, by following codes of conduct and principles which are seen as morally right and by being actively involved in the well-being of the community in which they operate. According to this view, companies cannot claim that they are socially responsible when they do not fulfil all of these responsibilities. Another more practical definition comes from MVO Nederland, an organisation that functions as a sort of CSR knowledge centre in the Netherlands—CSR means that companies, in addition to their efforts to make a profit, also take into account the effect of their actions on the environment (planet) and on human aspects within and outside the company (people). This means that companies have to find a balance between people, planet and profit.[4] Keijzers, Boons and van Daal (2002) point to the more strategic character of CSR, describing it as the process in which enterprises integrate ecological, economic and social aspects of their activities in a strategic way into their business.[5]

---

4 www.mvonederland.nl, accessed on 2 October 2009.
5 Despite the fact that these definitions have been drawn up mainly from the perspective of a company, they can be equally well applied to other organisations, not least to governments. In this way governments can take a stimulating role (for example as motivator, promoter, employer and customer). At the moment the focus is to stimulate companies to behave in a socially responsible way through sustainable procurement and making their business processes more sustainable. Essentially, this is about a distinction between policy (actions aimed at the external environment) and process (actions aimed at the internal environment). Therefore, for governments, CSR is both an end and a means.

According to many observers, CSR is to do with the core activities of companies. Several definitions implicitly or explicitly state that relationships with stakeholders, transparency and dialogue between the company and society are also part of CSR. Mintzberg, Ahlstrand and Lampel (1998) speak of the 'power school'—a stream in business thinking which states that a company has to take the environment of the organisation as well as its broad stakeholder group into account when developing a strategic policy. The concept environment in this case has a much broader and more pluralistic meaning than just the market, and relates more to the notion of institutional environment.

2.2.4 The essence of CSR

In order to gain a fuller understanding of what CSR means, it is necessary to take note of two related concepts:

- Responsibility

- Accountability

CSR means that companies take responsibility and are held accountable for any negative effects caused by them on the environment, on people and on society. These negative effects can be seen as a company's 'footprint'. Every company has a footprint—often more than one: an ecological footprint and a social footprint. The size and shape of the footprint indicates the nature and size of the effects of the activities undertaken by the company, the processes the company uses, the products it makes and/or the services it offers.

Both concepts are explained in the following paragraphs.

2.2.4.1 Responsibility

The notion of responsibility relates to 'responsibility according to' and to 'being responsible for'. 'Responsibility according to' relates to 'doing business according to the norms of responsibility as they exist in the society'. This interpretation emphasises that companies should do business according to norms formulated by their environment and the communities in which they operate (and of which they are part). These norms are behavioural rules or starting points for companies that are implicitly or explicitly part of, for instance, the national culture, laws and rules, and guidelines for responsible behaviour. Furthermore, the ambition of a company's management and the expectations of employees can play an important role here as these may enable or restrain the scope of an organisation's responsibility. According to this interpretation, the question that should be asked is: what is the meaning of social responsibility in the environment (both business and institutional environment) in which we operate and for our stakeholders?

Regarding 'being responsible for', CSR is interpreted by us as doing business while taking into account responsibility for society. This interpretation stresses that companies have a fundamental responsibility towards the environment and/or society in which they operate and of which they are an integral part. This raises a fundamental question, namely: what are the responsibilities of companies? Or: what exactly are companies responsible for?

2.2.4.2 Accountability

The concept of accountability relates to the notion that doing business involves being accountable towards society. The central idea behind this notion is that companies receive a mandate from society and their stakeholders to be able to do business; the so-called 'licence to operate'. This licence is provided conditionally, with the aim of earning trust. Companies are held accountable for their behaviour and responsibilities, they are expected to be transparent and to answer questions from their stakeholders. Hence, stakeholder dialogue is an important element of CSR.

Despite the fact that the concepts of responsibility and accountability are often seen as being similar, they are definitely not synonyms. They do have something in common, however: they both assume a certain degree of consciousness by organisations of their surroundings and

Did you know...

In 2008, Sweden was the first country in which 55 state-owned companies were required to report on their economic environmental and social performance. The Swedish government has made the guidelines of the Global Reporting Initiative (GRI) the mandatory model for such reporting.

environments, and acknowledge the idea that companies, as a part of an open system (can) influence (because of the effects they cause) and (can) be influenced (because they cause effects). At the same time these concepts also complement each other and provide an indication of the dynamics of CSR.

Of course, not all external effects caused by companies are negative. Expressing social or community involvement by means of sponsorships, employee volunteering or making use of the resources, people, networks or expertise of a company are all examples of positive external effects. Clearly, the creation of employment is also a positive effect of organisations (indeed this is a responsibility as well). Finally, it is important to make a distinction between conscious (intended) and unconscious (unintended) action in the context of an organisation causing effects. 'Intention'—meaning having the objective and aiming or striving for something—is an essential characteristic of CSR.

2.3 **CSR vs corporate community involvement**

A distinction is often made between CSR and corporate community involvement (CCI). These concepts are sometimes used as synonyms, even though they are substantially different concepts. While CSR can be defined along the lines of the notions of responsibility and accountability, CCI can be described as:

- The voluntary engagement of an organisation with society

- Often, but not necessarily, having a local community orientation

- Being expressed by the deployment of company (human, financial or other) resources

- For the purpose of actions that are not necessarily related to the core activities of an organisation

- Aiming to improve the quality of society or to strengthen or accelerate community development

- Without the precondition that it contributes to the economic performance of an organisation

The notion of 'quality of society' can be defined in very different ways. For example, an organisation engages in CCI when it donates money to a good cause or when it sponsors the local orchestra or sports club, but also when it enables employees to volunteer during work time, or when it enters a strategic partnership with an NGO. Moreover, in the context of doing business in developing countries, the creation of employment, enabling knowledge and skills development, and providing access to technology (as part of the emancipation and development of local people) can also be seen as forms of CCI.

Did you know...

In 2007 66% of Dutch companies donated money to good causes or sponsored events and other organisations, spending a total of €1.4 billion.

In general, CCI is about the use of an organisation's resources, such as knowledge and expertise, office supplies, facilities, money and networks for the purpose of improving the community. CCI does not necessarily need to have a relation with the 'people' aspects of CSR, but usually it deals more often with these aspects than with the 'planet' aspects. In any case, a trend can be observed that organisations are increasingly trying to give CCI a more strategic character: organisations have been seeking to forge relationships between involvement in the community and the core activities of the organisation, and to valorise the relationship between involvement in the community and economic performance. According to strategy guru Michael Porter (Porter and Kramer 2006), *this* is the essence of CSR: an organisation invests in its environment because of self-interest and should make strategic considerations when it wants to invest in community involvement. Within this idea lies the fundamental understanding of the interdependence of company and society and the interests they share.

2.3.1 Relationships between CSR and CCI

There are clear connections between CSR and CCI. CCI can be seen as the starting point of the CSR initiative of an organisation: the voluntary and optional character of CCI and the fact that CCI activities usually produce tangible results (in the sense that employees may be able to participate in them and experience them) and are usually relatively simple to realise, are a reason for many companies to see this as a first step in the field of CSR. Moreover, CCI can also serve as a sort of 'conductor' of CSR: because concrete CCI activities usually generate a lot of enthusiasm both within and outside an organisation, they can motivate staff and create support for the social initiatives of an organisation so accelerating the integration of CSR.

CCI, in the light of the aforementioned definition of CSR, can also be perceived as a manifestation of the creation of positive external effects by an organisation. The main difference with CSR, according to this criterion, is that CCI does not necessarily have to have a structural character. CCI activities may well be ad hoc, while CSR is essentially about a fundamental understanding or interpretation of the social responsibilities of an organisation. Both CCI and CSR are beyond legal compliance and are, in the end, an expression of the morality of organisations.

A third way to look at the relationship between CSR and CCI is by seeing CCI as a way to mitigate or compensate for the negative external effects of an organisation. A construction company that works on a project in a certain neighbourhood which causes noise and pollution can, for example, organise a community event prior to starting work in a bid to 'win hearts and minds' and head off complaints. At the beginning of the social event the company can provide information about the project, highlight any community benefits arising from it and detail the measures to be taken to reduce any nuisance or inconvenience. This example illustrates a very instrumental view of CCI in which the morality of the organisation or the intrinsic social engagement of the organisation is not an integral part per se.

Did you know...

As part of its HR policy, the city of Rotterdam gives its employees the opportunity to engage in voluntary work in the community. Enthusiasm is rewarded: if a civil servant wants to use a day of his or her holiday for volunteering, the city of Rotterdam matches this commitment by funding another day to be spent on the voluntary project.

Finally, CCI can be seen as a sub-set of CSR. Social engagement, illustrated by investment and involvement, is part of the social responsibility of companies. In line with the 3P idea, economic value becomes an increasingly important criterion for CCI activities. A more strategic use of CCI and the search for ways to practise CCI that suit the uniqueness (core activities and identity) of the organisation are also integral to this view of CCI. As will become clear from this book, this is the view of ISO 26000 on CCI: an integral part of CSR.

2.4 **CSR according to ISO 26000**

So far in this chapter the contents of, theories of and views on, the concept of CSR have been discussed. The majority viewpoint is that CSR means: taking responsibility for the negative effects of social and ecological footprints; increasing the positive effects of organisations on society; and being accountable and responsible for both negative and positive effects.

The final part of this chapter examines the ISO 26000 view on CSR.

2.4.1 Terminology

As noted in Chapter 1 (see §1.1.2) and the beginning of this chapter, the first thing that can be observed when looking at the interpretation of CSR within ISO 26000 is that the term 'social responsibility' (SR) is used instead of 'corporate social responsibility'. The main reason for this is that the guideline has not been developed to apply to large companies alone, but to be relevant for all types of organisations—including SMEs, local governments and NGOs. By choosing to use the term SR, ISO essentially introduces a new term, but its objective is clear. ISO defines CSR as a category within SR. Whether it was necessary to do this can be questioned. Within governmental organisations the use of the term 'corporate' is increasingly common. Moreover, the term 'social' may give the wrong impression, because this term can suggest that ISO 26000 does not deal with the 'green', environmental or 'planet' side of CSR (this is particularly the case for people whose first language is not English). This is an interesting observation in itself as the CSR debate is regularly dominated by environmental topics (such as climate change) with social sustainability themes being generally underexposed (de Lange and Koppens 2004).

Having said that, numerous environmental problems have social consequences (which is more support for the use of the term 'social'). This is illustrated by a quote from a recent report from the UN about the social effects stemming from climate change (UNDP 2008: 8):

> [. . .] failure will consign the poorest 40% of the world's population—some 2.6 billion people—to a future of diminished opportunity. It will exacerbate deep inequalities within countries. And it will undermine efforts to build a more inclusive pattern of globalisation, reinforcing the vast disparities between the 'haves' and the 'have nots'.

This also holds the other way around: ineffectively dealing with social challenges leads to negative environmental effects. For instance, poverty may hinder the use of more environmentally friendly technologies. Just as responsibility and accountability are two sides of the CSR coin, environmental effects and social effects are inextricably linked to each other.

2.4.2 The contents and the goal of social responsibility

Looking at the contents of the guideline, it is striking to observe that ISO 26000's definition of SR does not make a direct link between the social responsibilities of an organisation and the economic value of SR to that organisation. In other words: people and planet are uncoupled from profit. The guideline acknowledges that there is an economic value in managing one's policies towards people, the environment and society, but while the relationship between people, planet and profit is integral to the triple-bottom-line concept, this is not the case within ISO 26000.[6] SR in ISO 26000 seems mainly to have a moral orientation. What makes this even more interesting is that it can be argued that ISO 26000 breaks with the consensus view on CSR that has become dominant over the past few years which emphasises its business case.[7] On the other hand, ISO 26000 does not argue that CSR is merely about charity.

Did you know...

Research conducted by the Boston College for Corporate Citizenship showed that 70% of American managers see reputation as an important driver of CSR.[8]

ISO 26000 states that organisations should base their behaviour on standards, guidelines and codes of conduct that are acknowledged as being moral and justified in the context of specific organisations.[9]

Furthermore, the aim of SR, according to the guideline, is to contribute to sustainable development. The difference between sustainable development and SR is that SR has the organisation as its focus—not the world. However, both concepts are clearly linked to each other.[10] On the other hand, the symbiotic relationship between attention for

6 Indeed, the triple bottom line is not mentioned in ISO 26000 at all.
7 It is also interesting to note that making a profit is not explicitly seen as a social responsibility of companies by ISO 26000. Nothing in the document indicates that the definition of SR implies this. The only thing that can be said is that compliance with rules and regulations is an integral part of SR and that, as far as making a profit is a legal requirement for organisations (according to Milton Friedman's view), this does fall in the category of SR according to ISO 26000.
8 'The 2010 Corporate Social Responsibility Index'; www.bcccc.net/pdf/CSRIReport2010.pdf, accessed 15 March 2010.
9 The term 'social responsibility' is consequently defined as (ISO 2010: 3): '[. . .] responsibility of an organisation for the impacts of its decisions and activities on society and the environment, through transparent and ethical behaviour that (a) contributes to sustainable development, including health and the welfare of society, (b) takes into account the expectations of stakeholders, (c) is in compliance with applicable law and consistent with international norms of behaviour and (d) is integrated throughout the organisation and practised in its relationships'. It could be argued that, based on this passage, making a profit is an integral part of SR. The text under (d) 'integrated throughout the organisation' could indicate a symbiosis between the social responsibilities of an organisation and its profitability. However, this is never stated as such, let alone emphasised, within ISO 26000.
10 It should be noted that, despite the aim of ISO 26000 to create a uniform and clear conceptual framework, the term 'sustainability' has more than one definition in the guideline.

people and planet on the one hand and profit on the other is acknowledged by ISO 26000 in a number of sections. For example, regarding the actions that should be undertaken by companies in the field of occupational health and safety, the guideline states that the implementation of good health, safety and environmental standards should not be to the detriment of good business performance, but mutually beneficial. Similarly, providing access to technology (which is part of the related actions and expectations in the field of community involvement and development in the guideline) when it is *economically* viable to do so should enable an organisation to effect the transfer and diffusion of technology.

The introduction of ISO 26000 addresses the fact that it is becoming increasingly important for organisations to pay attention to SR themes because they are increasingly under scrutiny by their stakeholders, such as customers, employees, investors and society, and are being held accountable by them.[11] Furthermore, ISO 26000 stresses that the SR achievements of an organisation can positively influence its reputation, its ability to attract and retain employees and customers, raise employee morale, create organisational pride, improve the commitment and productivity of employees, generate better evaluations from stockholders and analysts, and sweeten its relationships with other companies, suppliers, governments and the media.

At several places in the guideline we are pointed to the potential advantages of SR, such as improving risk management, costs savings from more efficient use of water and energy, avoidance of conflicts with customers and contributing to the quality of society as a whole (which, in turn, positively influences the performance of the organisation).

2.4.3 Willingness, effect and integration

SR, according to ISO 26000, has to do with the *willingness* of an organisation to take up its responsibilities, its awareness of the effects of its activities and decisions on society and its environment, and its capacity to act upon these in a structural way. This is the essential characteristic of SR.[12] So, according to

---

11 That is why the guideline states (ISO 2010: vi): 'An organisation's performance in relation to the society in which it operates and to its impact on the environment has become a critical part of measuring its overall performance and its ability to continue operating effectively. This is, in part, a reflection of the growing recognition of the need for ensuring healthy ecosystems, social equity and good organisational governance.'

12 Therefore, SR means that an organisation displays (ISO 2010: 6): '[t]ransparent and ethical behaviour that contributes to sustainable development, is in compliance

ISO 26000, SR is much more than mere compliance with laws and rules. This view is consistent with most (modern) views on CSR.

To be able to determine its social responsibilities, it is important for an organisation to distinguish between the effects of its activities and decisions on the interests and expectations of stakeholders and on the interests and expectations of society as a whole. When determining the social responsibilities of an organisation, it should take into account all these aspects.

Also, the importance of integrating SR in an organisation—making sure the organisation truly 'breathes' its social responsibilities—is emphasised by the guideline. Only by means of deep integration of SR can the possible and real effects of the activities, decisions and day-to-day practices of an organisation be addressed properly. Making compliance with social responsibilities part of the organisation's day-to-day tasks is seen as the most important behavioural change for an organisation by ISO 26000. In addition, an organisation should be aware of the fact that the interests and expectations of stakeholders and society can change.[13]

2.5 **ISO 26000 and CCI**

As discussed earlier, CCI is seen as an integral part of SR by ISO 26000. In fact, an entire core subject is dedicated to CCI: 'Community involvement and development' (see Chapter 6). According to ISO 26000, CCI is not restricted to identifying and engaging stakeholders affected by an organisation's activities. It is also about supporting the development of a community and the ability of an organisation to identify and acknowledge the value of its community. CCI should be based on an acknowledgement of the fact that an organisation is a stakeholder in the community that has the same or similar interests as that community. Consequently, this is how CCI is defined in ISO 26000.[14]

---

with applicable law and consistent with international norms of behaviour. It also implies that social responsibility is integrated throughout the organisation, practised in its relationships and takes into account the interests of stakeholders.'

13 'The elements of social responsibility reflect the expectations of society at a particular time, and are therefore liable to change. As society's concerns change, its expectations of organisations also change to reflect those concerns' (ISO 2010: 5).

14 'An organisation's proactive outreach to the community. It is aimed at preventing and solving problems, fostering partnerships with local organisations and stakeholders and aspiring to be a good organisational citizen of the community. It does not replace the need for taking responsibility for impacts on society and environment. Organisations contribute to their communities through their participation

One of the underlying principles of CCI, according to ISO 26000, is that an organisation should view itself as an integral part of the community or communities in which it operates, being aware of, and recognising, the culture and history of the community (ISO 2010: 61). When an organisation engages in a CCI initiative it should also consider supporting public policies aimed at community development. A shared vision and understanding of priorities and partnerships maximises the organisation's contribution to sustainable development, as well as its ability to contribute to social well-being and quality of life, according to ISO 26000. ISO 26000 clearly puts forward the link between SR and CCI, noting that socially responsible behaviour enhances community development (ISO 2010: 61).

Creating employment, technological development and access to technology, social investments aimed at increasing prosperity and income by means of local economic development, investment in education, cultural preservation and offering access to healthcare all fall under the core subject 'Community involvement and development'. Philanthropy also falls under this core subject, according to ISO 26000, but the guideline adds that it is not a substitute for other types of CCI activities. In other words: philanthropy alone does not equate to CCI. Only when a financial donation is combined with another CCI activity may an organisation state that it conducts business in a socially responsible way.

2.6 **Final words**

For the remainder of this book it is important to keep in mind some of the key concepts we have discussed here, such as the idea of an organisation's footprint, and of responsibility and accountability. When these concepts are taken as a starting point it becomes clear that the 'vague' concept of CSR is not that vague at all. As well as the responsibility to make a profit (or, in the case of not-for-profit organisations, a responsibility for their continuity), organisations also have responsibilities for people and planet in order to contribute to sustainable development—that is the essence of the role that SR plays, according to ISO 26000. However, the guideline does not explicitly link an organisation's

---

in and support for civil institutions and through involvement in networks of groups and individuals that constitute civil society. Community involvement also helps organisations to familiarise themselves with community needs and priorities, so that the organisation's developmental and other efforts are compatible with those of the community and society' (ISO 2010: 63).

responsibilities for people and planet to profit and so breaks with the win–win scenario that has been emphasised in several recent contributions (see, for example, Porter and Kramer 2006), such as this from the book *Buried Treasure* (Wall 2008: 8):

> So implementing CSR is not about companies engaging in charity; on the contrary, it is about companies actively pursuing their self-interests but in the process creating value for society.

It is characteristic of such views that the social responsibilities of companies are almost seen as an unintended side-effect. Such opinions are characterised by the denial of an inherent morality for business. Perhaps this has been necessary to let CSR come of age and to help it evolve into a mainstream business concept. ISO 26000 brings the morality of business—and, indeed, of all organisations—back to centre stage.

To get a better and more detailed understanding of the guideline, the next chapter discusses the background, characteristics and structure of ISO 26000.

Interlude I
SR in practice: motivations, manifestations and results

I.1 **Introduction**

SR manifests itself in many ways and with many different results in the day-to-day lives of organisations. Earlier in this book, we stated that this 'pluralism' fits well with the way ISO 26000 views SR: every organisation has its own interpretation of SR, based on an organisation-specific context and because of its own motivations. In other words every organisation has its own, unique SR profile.

In this Interlude a number of common drivers for SR will be discussed, followed by the manifestations of SR (what does SR 'look like' in practice?). The Interlude ends with some examples of outcomes and results that organisations can achieve as a result of their SR efforts. The focus here is on the business or economic value of SR for an organisation—not on the sustainability aspects (decreasing negative impacts on society and environment).

I.2 **Motivations**

There are many motivations for organisations to engage with SR. Almost all of these can be distilled down to either 'We do SR because it is mandatory', 'We do SR because it is the right thing to do', or 'We do SR because it pays'.

I.2.1 We do SR because it is mandatory

More and more organisations feel the pressure of society, clients, consumers or other stakeholders to develop ways to deal with SR-related issues. The attitude of organisations that engage with 'SR because it is mandatory' is often reactive, defensive and compliance-oriented. The organisation does not undertake action until an explicit question or demand arises or when a (minimum) requirement is set by law and the organisation complies with that (minimum) requirement. One example here is requirements in the field of sustainable procurement that governments and, increasingly, companies set.

I.2.2 We do SR because it is the right thing to do

In this category, an organisation engages in SR because its leaders, management and/or employees think that it has a role as part of society in general, is dependent upon society and should have a responsibility to society. The organisation has similar rights and duties to those of individuals and hence it should have knowledge of the effects it has on society and be responsible for these effects. This motivation often originates from personal beliefs and a feeling that it is important to give back to society. Essentially, this is moral motivation for SR.

I.2.3 We do SR because it pays

Organisations here are motivated by the fact that there are good business reasons—a business case—for engaging with SR. This might be because they see market advantages in new products and services serving sustainability. Cost reductions also fall within this category. The organisation may be convinced of the benefits of energy efficiency, for example. The organisation asks 'What's in it for us?' and considers the business and economic value of its SR initiatives as the paramount concern. This is about gaining the so-called 'win–win' or, from the perspective of the triple bottom line, a 'win–win–win' situation.

A 2007 study conducted by EIM Business & Policy Research (Hoevenagel 2007) on SR among larger SMEs commissioned by the Netherlands

Environmental Assessment Agency showed that 41% of the group that engages in SR does this because it 'pays off', 38% because it is 'the right thing to do' and 12% because it is 'mandatory'. The remaining 9% had other reasons for engaging with SR. One of those reasons was because 'it is inspiring'.

Another report, from the European Stakeholder Forum (2004), suggested the following reasons for SMEs to invest in SR:

- Attracting, maintaining and developing motivated, talented and devoted employees

- Attracting and maintaining clients (both consumers and business clients)

- Being a 'good neighbour'

- Answering to demands from banks and insurance companies

- Reputational considerations, both regarding internal and external stakeholders

- Realising cost reductions and efficiencies

- Network possibilities

- Innovation and differentiation

- Anticipating future laws and rules

I.3 **Manifestations**

A lot of uncertainty surrounds the term 'SR'. This is understandable, as it can mean quite different

Did you know...

The PricewaterhouseCoopers Sustainability barometer of September 2009 reported that one-fifth of Dutch companies decided to get more involved in sustainable business because of the economic crisis.[1]

Did you know...

The PricewaterhouseCoopers Sustainability barometer of September 2009 showed that 89% of Dutch companies think that SR leads to a better reputation which, consequently, has a positive effect on profits. In addition, 43% felt that a motivated employee leads to increased productivity, 39% thought that the company becomes a more attractive employer and 30% believed that by engaging with SR other investors and business partners could be attracted or new markets opened.[2]

---

1 Anders Bekken blog, 13 October 2009;
   www.stichtingmilieunet.nl/andersbekekenblog/duurzaam/de-pricewaterhouseco
   opers-duurzaamheidbarometer-duurzaamheid-heeft-een-vaste-positie-veroverd.
   html, accessed 19 March 2011.
2 Ibid.

things for different organisations depending on their activities, sector and geographical location. A textile factory will have vastly different concerns to a public policy agency; a commercial high-street bank cannot be compared to a consumer electronics company. That is both the key strength and weakness of SR—many different interpretations are both possible and plausible. The result is that it can be difficult to get a good view of the SR activities of an organisation.

SR appears in many different forms and these are dependent on idiosyncratic interpretations, the opportunities organisations see in SR, and the expectations that stakeholders and society have regarding the organisation. Some see SR as an ethical 'test' for managerial decision-making, while others see SR as the next step in business excellence. One organisation may focus on the marketing possibilities of SR, while another sees SR as an instrument to recalibrate HR policies. In conclusion, many different manifestations of SR can be found in an organisation (see Box I.1).

Box I.1 **Appearances and manifestations of SR**

- Codes of conduct
- CO_2 reduction programme
- Fair Trade products
- Healthy food in the canteen
- Environmental management systems
- Reputation management
- Diversity policy
- Use of green energy
- Business principles
- Employee volunteering
- Reduction of materials usage
- Sustainable innovation
- HSEQ management
- Sustainable building
- Partnerships with NGOs
- Employing disabled employees
- Water and energy savings
- Integrity policy
- Use of movement sensors
- Purchasing electric cars
- Community involvement
- Sponsoring a local sports club
- Stakeholder consultations
- Installation of solar panels

I.4 **Results**

The results and outcomes of engaging with SR are obviously closely related to the organisation's motivations, although intention and effect are not always the same. Research on the relationship between the level of engagement with SR and an organisation's profitability does not portray a clear picture: SR *can* offer economic value for an organisation, but there isn't a correlation per se. An explanation for this is that it is very hard to properly identify the effects of investments in SR. How does community involvement affect the bottom line? How does the adoption of a code of ethics save the company money? A better starting point to get an idea of the potential value of SR is to think of profit as a multidimensional concept which includes indirect profits or long-term effects. For example, SR can contribute to customer loyalty, which may well lead to reduced marketing costs. A similar argument can be made for the benefit an organisation gains through attracting and retaining a motivated workforce. Increasing the innovative capacity of an organisation can also be seen as a benefit of SR.

Recent research conducted by Cochius and Moratis (2009) commissioned by the Dutch Directorate General of Public Works and Water Management among SR champions in both the Netherlands and abroad showed that these organisations mainly engage in SR because it adds value—SR directly and indirectly contributes to the bottom-line of the organisation. Some of the benefits reported were:

- *Direct cost savings*. By simply using less energy, materials and reducing waste, decreasing the use of fuel and saving water, costs can be cut. For example, TNT has the ambition to become the world's first mail and courier company to operate in a carbon-neutral way. Part of the programme to realise this, which is known as 'Planet Me', is training employees to change their driving behaviour. This training not only leads to a reduction in fuel usage and thus in the CO_2 emissions of the company's vehicles, but also to a considerable fall in the number of accidents. Hence, TNT saved costs in two ways.

- *Better labour market positioning*. Research has shown that employees, especially talented, young professionals with high potential, value the way in which an organisation fulfils its role in society—and the SR champions appeared to experience that as well. Moreover, (future) employees generally expect an organisation that takes its sustainability impact seriously also takes good care of its employees.

- *More market opportunities*. The experience of SR champions suggests that they were able to create more market opportunities by offering sustainable and innovative products and services. In the Netherlands alone, there are an estimated 1.7 million consumers prepared to buy green or sustainable products.[3] This does not take into account the business-to-business market. The Dutch government has also

3 'De Cultural Creative: 1,7 miljoen Cultural Creatives in Nederland', marketresponse; www.marketresponse.nl/themas/duurzaamheid/cultural-creatives/de-cultural-creative, accessed 17 April 2011.

developed sophisticated guidelines for sustainable procurement and tenders. SMEs are also experiencing a growth in the number of questionnaires regarding sustainability from large multinational customers. The simple conclusion is that there are more than enough market opportunities.

- *Reputation.* Engaging with and communicating about SR may well result in opportunities for improving the reputation of an organisation. Caution is advised here. Greenwashing—over-emphasising the sustainability attributes of a product or service, or focusing on the sustainability benefits of one product when others are damaging to the environment or society—can backfire and have completely the opposite effect on reputation. Still, when an organisation has developed a solid SR strategy, it should communicate this to clients, suppliers, investors, (future) employees and society.

- *Increasing employee pride and engagement.* Research among SR champions shows that SR may result in higher levels of employee engagement and organisational pride in two ways. First, engagement can be increased by investing in the health, safety, development and education of employees. Second, employees often appreciate the opportunity to contribute to a better world during work time.

- *Improved relationship management.* Building relationships with like-minded people also illustrates the value of SR for relationship management. Organisations that see the world through the lens of sustainability will likely recognise opportunities and challenges at an early stage. In terms of relationship management this can yield better understanding, trust and new opportunities for cooperation with clients and others.

The results of SR as described above are not exhaustive. SR can add value to different areas or functions of an organisation. It can also add value for stakeholders. This broad perspective offers a visionary organisation the space and opportunity to engage in SR in its own, organisation-specific way.

3

ISO 26000: background, characteristics and structure

3.1 **Introduction**

The previous chapter provided a first look at ISO 26000, what it is and what it is about. The main focus so far has been on the ISO 26000 view on (C)SR and the target audience of the guideline. In this chapter, the guideline will be discussed in more detail and its background, features and characteristics will be described and explained in order to obtain a better and more detailed idea of what ISO 26000 comprises and aims for.

This chapter starts with the reasons why ISO 26000 was developed in the first place and continues with the observation that in recent years a veritable labyrinth of SR guidelines, norms and standards has come into existence. An organisation has to be very well equipped in order to find its way through this labyrinth and can easily develop a certain degree of scepticism for such guidelines and standards. Still, such standards and guidelines are important. This chapter stresses that importance and makes several distinctions between these standards and guidelines. Subsequently, ISO 26000 is categorised by means of a typology and the scope and aims of the guideline are discussed. There is special attention for the opportunity ISO 26000 offers for an organisation-specific interpretation of SR in this chapter. ISO 26000, it is argued, is a guideline that is suitable for next-generation SR—SR 2.0. The final part of this chapter deals with the outline and structure of the guideline itself and explains the anatomy of ISO 26000 in a nutshell.

3.2 **Why ISO 26000 was developed**

The development of ISO 26000 started in 2005. In previous years, many discussions had taken place and preparations were made to reach a decision on whether or not it was desirable to develop this guideline at all and, if so, in which direction its development should take place.

The need to develop a SR guideline was first raised in 2001 by the Committee on Consumer Policy of ISO (ISO/COPOLCO), after which the Ad Hoc Group on CSR was founded in 2003. This Ad Hoc Group took stock of all known worldwide SR initiatives and issues. After positive advice from a multi-stakeholder conference in 2004, the decision to develop ISO 26000 by means of both a democratic process and input from developing countries was finally made in January 2005.

As is clear from previous chapters, ISO 26000 has multiple objectives. One objective, for example, is to support organisations in defining their social responsibilities and acting in accordance with these responsibilities in order to contribute to sustainable development. Another objective is to increase the credibility of SR claims. Such objectives are already good motivations for the development of ISO 26000 in themselves, but more specific reasons for the development of a global SR guideline exist as well.

First, despite many initiatives in the field of SR, such as the development of standards, codes, norms and guidelines, an international, broadly oriented, comprehensive, and overarching SR guideline issued by a well-known authority was not yet available. The guidelines of the Sustainability Integrated Guidelines for Management (SIGMA) project,[1] launched in 1999, could have been an interesting competitor for ISO 26000, but these never received broad recognition, let alone application. Many standards, of course, focus on a

---

1 SIGMA was a UK initiative. In 2003 the guidelines were updated for the last time. More information can be found at www.projectsigma.co.uk.

specific area of SR, such as SA8000 and labour standards and the ISO 14001 on environmental management. ISO 26000 has the ambition to be a comprehensive SR guideline that will enable all organisations to define their social responsibilities. The guideline aims to find a combination of—and build a bridge between—compliance with laws and rules by organisations on the one hand, and, on the other hand, an open, idiosyncratic approach to defining corporate responsibilities based on many well-known reference documents, without frustrating creativity and development.[2] Moreover, ISO 26000 tries to make the connection with existing and familiar systems, and aims to offer a framework for the (practical) translation of international treaties, agreements and conventions in the field of SR. ISO 26000 probably makes the conundrum many organisations have about SR a little easier to solve, because the guideline contributes to obtaining a comprehensive overview, and hence makes it easier for organisations to engage in SR.[3]

3.2.1 Why ISO?

An interesting question is why ISO—of all organisations—would be the right body to develop this international guideline. Is ISO actually the proper organisation to do so? It can be argued that ISO is not—and in the past years several critics have made that case (as well as why it is a bad idea to develop a global SR standard in the first place). ISO's experience with the topic of SR is very limited and the SR guideline could easily be mistakenly linked with a norm for a management system. There is clearly confusion here. Furthermore, it has been argued that a SR guideline should not be associated with the ISO label, because this would not benefit the adoption of it. ISO 26000 would, analogous with OHSAS 18001 (which has not been developed within the ISO context), for example, perhaps be better off if it carried an indication such as 'SR 26000' as ISO does not always has a positive connotation. On the other hand, the ISO organisation offers several important advantages for the development of a global SR guideline, from the perspective of the organisation's objectives. For instance, ISO is one of the few organisations that is broadly acknowledged internationally—it is known all around the world and the organisation's activities are of importance to every single individual in the world. It can also be expected that ISO 26000 will receive visibility in many organisations that already work with other ISO management systems but which have not yet engaged meaningfully with SR. The previously mentioned

---

2 See also www.iso.org/sr.
3 More aims and functions of ISO 26000 can be found in §3.4.2.

research by Brandsma *et al.* (2009) confirms this: between 55% and 60% of the respondents that work with an ISO-certified or related management system standards are considering applying ISO 26000 in their organisations. In addition, ISO has extensive experience with the development and dissemination of standards and has the organisational capacity to do this. Significantly, the development of ISO 26000 has been based on the largest multi-stakeholder process that has ever been organised. Hundreds of experts from numerous countries have cooperated in the process. The amount of work, research and discussion that this stakeholder diversity of opinions and insights has generated is truly unparalleled. The aim has been to strive for mutual and universal basic definitions, principles, working methods and guidelines—an international standard, written in (relatively) straightforward language. People who are not SR specialists can also understand and work with the guideline. In addition, the guideline is applicable to all organisations, in all countries, in all stages of development, all sectors and does not conflict with other SR standards or demands—it has no intention of replacing these.[4]

3.3 **The SR jungle: a labyrinth of codes, norms, standards and guidelines**

With the developments in the field of social responsibility of organisations—and the increasing importance of accountability and transparency in reporting an organisation's own SR achievements—numerous guidelines, standards and codes have been developed. Some of these have been developed by independent organisations, others by NGOs or by companies and yet others by standardisation organisations such as ISO. SR has also been growing in terms of the number of topics it covers. For example, privacy protection, information protection and dealing with (personal) information in a responsible way has become an important SR theme for companies operating in the IT sector and the banking sector. With this, the ISO 27000 series about information security has become a relevant standard within the context of SR for many companies. Hundreds of SR-related codes, guidelines, standards and management systems have been developed. We might refer to this as the SR jungle. Because of this jungle and because of the fact that there are often not clear

---

4 '[This International Standard] is intended to promote common understanding in the field of social responsibility, and to complement other instruments and initiatives for social responsibility and not to replace them' (ISO 2010: 1).

boundaries between where one code ends and another starts, duplication of requirements, red tape and information overload, a certain weariness has developed among (potential) users. Clearly, this is an unusual jungle—one that the world is better off without.

3.3.1 Why they exist—and why they are important

However, there are good reasons for organisations to develop and adopt such codes, standards and guidelines. They have been developed with the aim of creating some order in the existing chaos—organisations like to have clarity about the SR themes they should be considering and what is expected from them. The contents of codes, standards and guidelines are often a reflection of generally accepted and desirable behaviour, and they contain both minimum requirements and best practices. One of the other aims is to make SR practical, easy-to-use and to offer key points—sometimes in the form of principles that organisations should follow or adopt, but also in the form of actions and initiatives that an organisation could undertake. They translate the expectations of society, minimum requirements and best practices into so-called action perspectives. They are instruments to create a sustainable way of doing business. In addition, codes, standards and guidelines are good instruments for organisations to demonstrate that they comply with certain requirements and that they account for their social responsibilities. Therefore, they can build confidence or enhance the credibility of the statements and the SR performance of an organisation. Also, those organisations that use codes, standards and guidelines can make employees (more) aware of SR and the attempts of their employers to be a good citizen.

ISO 26000 is the next (and definitely not the last) addition to these codes, standards and guidelines. The difference may be in its potential. It *could* become the leading authoritative, integral standard for SR.

3.3.2 Distinguishing between types of standards

It is not always clear what the distinction is between codes, guidelines, standards and management systems, and the terms are regularly used interchangeably. The usage of terms such as marks, labels and certificates does not help in making a clear distinction between these different instruments. No matter what the exact differences are, the SR jungle hides a lot of species that, at least for a large part, have many things in common or even refer to the same topics or requirements.[5] What they have in common, is that they have developed themselves into acknowledged standards that help organisations engage in (often in sub-areas of) SR. A second thing that they all have in common is that they are all voluntary, meaning that there is no legal entity that requires their use or application. A third common characteristic is that they offer starting points (and to a certain degree function as practical guides) for repeatable good practice.

In *The Corporate Responsibility Code Book* Deborah Leipziger (2003) describes a standard as a set of principles, codes of conduct or process systems, developed by a third party. Its implementation should result in a certain level of performance that is established beforehand—either by the standard itself or by the organisation that implements or audits the standard. Generally, a distinction is made between process standards, performance standards, principle standards and basic standards. Process standards describe the procedures that should be present within an organisation in order to execute certain activities. This can mean organising a stakeholder dialogue or publishing a sustainability report. A good example of a process standard is AA1000SES, which is aimed at creating excellent stakeholder engagement. Performance standards, on the other hand, describe what an organisation should or should not do, such as paying a certain level of wages or preventing discrimination at work. These are more or less minimum standards for socially responsible behaviour. Examples of this are the OECD guidelines for multinational enterprises and the working condition conventions of the ILO (International Labour Organisation). Process standards and performance standards are, however, not mutually exclusive categories. There are several 'hybrid standards' which combine both process and performance, of which SA8000 (with a focus on labour conditions in the supply chain) is an example. Principle standards describe principles that should be at the core of organisations' activities, although they do not specify how those principles can be achieved or how acting in accordance with those principles can be evaluated. Examples of these include the UN Global Compact (see Annex 5) and the Global Sullivan Principles. Basic standards aim to lay the foundation for a new focus area, and describe what the best practice in a certain area is. Besides these kinds of standards, sometimes even a fifth kind of standard is distinguished, namely a certification standard. These are standards for which certificates can be obtained for operating in accordance with them, as determined by an independent third party, such as an auditor. Examples of these

---

5 For this reason, from now on, the term 'standard' will be used.

kinds of standards are management system standards such as ISO 14001 for environmental management.

Making a distinction between standards on the basis of these criteria can be useful in terms of comparison, for understanding how they can be complementary to each other and in assessing how they compete with each other. Standards can be classified according to:[6]

- Their focus or goal (whether they focus on process, performance and/or principles)

- The way in which they have been developed (unilateral, bilateral or multilateral)

- Their scope (whether they deal with human rights, labour conditions, the environment, etc.)

- Their stakeholder orientation (whether they concentrate on, for example, employees, investors, consumers or on multiple stakeholders)

Even though SR standards can be categorised and distinguished from each other, they often do not stand alone—there is a clear relationship between them. Several standards refer to each other, sometimes because each individual standard only covers one element of the range of SR themes, and the same stakeholder groups have participated in developing several standards. Because the GRI (Global Reporting Initiative) for example, has been adopted and supported by the UN, there is a clear link between the GRI guidelines and the UN's Global Compact. Although GRI does not offer monitoring instruments or indications on how companies can act according to the principles of the Global Compact, the GRI guidelines can be used to advise companies on how they can illustrate their compliance with the Global Compact in their annual reports. SA 8000 has been developed with the idea of being able to be integrated into ISO systems. Leipziger (2003: 19) states:

> There is no single code or standard, no panacea that will lead to corporate responsibility. Each company is different, with its own challenges, corporate culture, unique set of stakeholders and management systems. Corporate responsibility is a journey for which there is no single map but hundreds of guides, codes and standards: maps that can be combined in new ways for different journeys.

The idea of a journey is also applicable to the evolution of standards, as witnessed by the many revisions and versions of some standards, such as ISO

6 Ibid.

9001 and AA1000. The process of standard development is at least as important as the standards themselves. It is a mechanism to involve different stakeholder perspectives.

The ambition of ISO 26000, as a generic, overarching SR guideline, is to enable its integration with any existing SR or CSR standard. The next paragraph will deal with the background and aims of ISO 26000 in more detail.

3.4 **A closer look at ISO 26000**

The prefix 'ISO' may distort people's perceptions about ISO 26000. ISO's association with norms, obligations, procedures, rules and handbooks is almost inescapable. And not withstanding their usefulness or necessity, they are not the most inspiring or attractive aspects of the organisation's reputation. Moreover, 'ISO' creates an association with certifiable management systems, especially due to the prominence of ISO 9001 and ISO 14001. The problematic thought of 'certifying for certification purposes' and the effort it takes an organisation to get everything in order to successfully go through an external audit to receive a certificate, has determined ISO's image to a large extent. ISO 26000 is, however, neither a norm nor is it certifiable.

Earlier in this book we explained how SR is defined within ISO 26000. It has become clear that ISO 26000 has a moral orientation, even though the guideline does not ignore the possible financial value of SR. The guideline is characterised by its level of ambition. Over 400 experts in the field of SR and in sub-areas such as CSR from dozens of countries have worked on the guideline. These people reflected six stakeholder groups: consumers; government; industry; trade unions; NGOs; and service, support, research and other organisations (SSROs, which also include consultants and universities). The development process started in 2005 and has been led by the Brazilian and the Swedish standardisation institutes. The most important ambition: to develop *the* overarching, global SR guideline.

But what kind of a guideline is ISO 26000 exactly? And what guidance does it provide? These questions will be answered in the coming paragraphs. For additional information on ISO 26000, and some of the key myths and misunderstandings about it, the reader is referred to Interludes II and III.

3.4.1 What type of guideline is ISO 26000 and what is its scope?

As has been stated several times before in this book: ISO 26000 is a *guideline*. As such, within the ISO terminology, it finds itself in the category of 'International Standards'. Within this category, ISO 26000 is a special kind of standard, a so-called 'Guidance Standard'. A Guidance Standard can be used by organisations on a voluntary basis. Such a guideline offers recommendations and advice about activities that organisations can undertake in a certain field.

By characterising ISO 26000 based on the distinctions that have been discussed above, it is clear that this is an extensive guideline with the aim of becoming an overarching and universally applicable guideline. ISO 26000 includes background and developments in the field of SR and sustainable development, underlying SR principles, advice on creating stakeholder engagement, numerous SR core subjects and SR issues, offers suggestions for the implementation of SR in existing strategies, systems, ways of working and processes of organisations, including communication about and enhancing the credibility of SR commitments and achievements, and refers to other standards that organisations can use in concordance with it. ISO 26000 aims to be a guideline that outlines all an organisation's social responsibilities and addresses many SR themes. ISO 26000 hence wants to be useful for all types of organisations, irrespective of their size, sector, geographic location and irrespective of their stage of SR implementation.[7]

The research that was conducted by Brandsma *et al.* in 2009 showed that most organisations that indicated an interest in ISO 26000 are still at an early stage in terms of SR implementation (see Fig. 3.1). For all of these organisations ISO 26000 is an applicable source of guidance as an introduction into SR and SR subject areas and as a guideline to structure their SR activities. Organisations that have already developed SR strategies and initiatives are more likely to apply ISO 26000 to increase the credibility of the own SR claims, e.g. by referring to the guideline in their SR communications.

---

7 'Recognising that organisations are at various stages of understanding and integrating social responsibility, this International Standard is intended for use by those beginning to address social responsibility, as well as those more experienced with its implementation' (ISO 2010: vi).

Figure 3.1 **Stages of SR implementation**

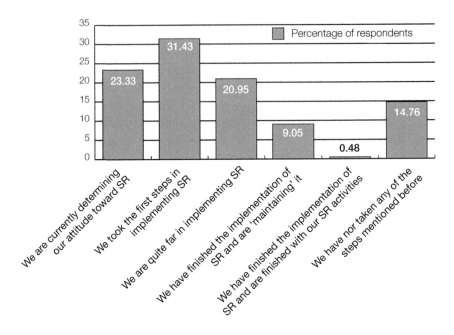

ISO 26000 emphasises the importance of results and the improvement of performance—continuous improvement, for instance, is one of the basic tenets of this guideline as well. Also ISO 26000's origin as the work of a huge range of stakeholders has perhaps unsurprisingly resulted in a very strong emphasis on stakeholder identification, dialogue and engagement. The guideline identifies the entire range of possible stakeholders of organisations. At the same time, organisations, guided by ISO 26000, are encouraged to define and describe their own social responsibilities and reduce the negative effects of their actions and decisions on people, planet, society and their stakeholders. Therefore, ISO 26000 can be defined as a hybrid standard: it contains elements of a process standard, of a performance standard (even though, despite recommending compliance with certain minimum achievements in a select number of SR core subjects and an emphasis on continuous improvement, it does not specify concrete achievement levels), a principles standard and a basic standard. What it is clearly not is a certification standard.

3.4.2 Objectives of ISO 26000

The most important aim of ISO 26000 is helping organisations to contribute to sustainable development.[8] Organisations are encouraged by the guideline to undertake activities that go beyond what is required by law. Compliance with laws and rules, however, is a fundamental aspect of the social responsibilities of any organisation.

When looking at what the guideline asks organisations to aim for, in conjunction with what information is actually documented in ISO 26000, at least the following functions can be ascribed to it:

- ISO 26000 advises: the guideline provides suggestions to organisations, and offers guidance for determining their social responsibilities

- ISO 26000 prescribes: the guidance specifies numerous guidelines, specifies many actions that organisations should undertake and describes what expectations they should meet

- ISO 26000 structures: the guideline offers organisations insight into how they can structure their SR initiatives and how to deal with SR implementation step by step in a structured way

- ISO 26000 explains: the guideline defines concepts and principles, and explains these in background information

- ISO 26000 harmonises: the guideline lays a foundation for a uniform and universal conceptual framework and specifies SR building blocks by means of SR core subjects

- ISO 26000 integrates: the guideline provides an umbrella for the application of other, existing standards in the field of SR

- ISO 26000 creates order: the guideline maps existing standards in the field of SR and offers an overview based on the contents (the core subjects) and process (implementation) of SR

- ISO 26000 reflects: the guideline offers consideration of and appraisal frameworks for many SR subjects

- ISO 26000 stimulates: the guideline encourages organisations to do business in a more socially responsible way by using the guideline and by offering space for organisations to interpret the guideline according to their own context and spheres of influence

8 'This International Standard is intended to assist organisations in contributing to sustainable development' (ISO 2010: 1).

- ISO 26000 inspires: the guideline attempts to enthuse organisations in engaging with SR by emphasising the broader importance of organisations in realising a sustainable society

It is explicitly *not* an aim of ISO 26000 to replace codes already in existence but, rather, to complement them. The guideline aims to be a framework in which already existing standards can be applied. It is also not an aim to replace laws and rules nor to change organisations' legal obligations.[9]

ISO 26000 intends to give organisations the possibility to formulate an organisation-specific interpretation of SR, based on the SR foundation it provides. ISO 26000 also crucially enables organisations to develop their own, unique SR profile. Because this idea of a SR profile plays an important role in ISO 26000, and because it characterises a new generation of SR, this idea will be discussed in the following sections.

3.5 **SR 2.0: a new generation of SR**

Probably the most important characteristic of ISO 26000 is that it offers the possibility for an organisation-specific interpretation of SR. In fact, this is encouraged by the guideline and seen as an organisation's own responsibility.[10]

This idea can, in our view, best be characterised as a new generation of SR—SR 2.0.[11] SR 2.0 is not about completing checklists in order for organisations to determine or fulfil their social responsibility ('you tell us what we are supposed to comply with'), but is about organisations developing their own

---

9 '[I]t is not intended to provide a basis for legal actions, complaints, defences or other claims in any international, domestic or other proceeding, nor is it intended to be cited as evidence of the evolution of customary international law' (ISO 2010: 1).

10 'In applying this International Standard it is advisable that an organisation take into consideration societal, environmental, legal, cultural, political and organisational diversity, as well as differences in economic conditions, while being consistent with international norms of behaviour' (ISO 2010: 1); '[I]t is an individual organisation's responsibility to identify which issues are relevant and significant for the organisation to address, through its own considerations and through dialogue with stakeholders' (ISO 2010: vi).

11 The addition 2.0 is used here in analogy with an improved version of an IT application, such as the internet. Web 2.0 represents a new type of use of the internet, of which, among others, active involvement of users in the development of the internet, interaction between users and the use of social networks are defining elements.

2.0: a new generation

There have been various authors who have construed new approaches to SR as new generations or 2.0 versions of SR. What 2.0 is depends on one's starting point. In his recent book *The Age of Responsibility: CSR 2.0 and the New DNA of Business* SR expert Wayne Visser (2011) argues that the new-generation movement CSR 2.0 goes beyond philanthropy and public relations. CSR 2.0 is about a more interactive, stakeholder-centred model of SR. It departs from an old SR paradigm in which SR has never moved to the core of business operations, was seen as a bolt-on or plug-in by companies and in which there wasn't a clear link between social responsibilities and business profitability. In Visser's view, CSR 2.0 is based on the principles of creativity, scalability, responsiveness, glo-cality and circularity and forms the basis for a new DNA model of responsible enterprise, which is built around value creation, good governance, societal contribution and environmental integrity.

In the book *Sustainability 2.0: Networking Enterprises and Citizens to Face World Challenges* by Ernesto Peborgh (2008), this new generation is explained from a more technological perspective which is built around the development of new, interactive internet applications such as social media. Behind this, there is a paradigm of participation, cooperation and transparency. Sustainability 2.0 profits from collaboration and collective intelligence empowered by new technologies and social networks to find balance in social and economic development through dynamic participation of citizens and companies.

In this book, we see ISO 26000 as a guidance for SR 2.0—a model of SR that is tailored to an organisation's specific context. SR 2.0 allows (or, better, urges) organisations to build idiosyncratic interpretations of their social responsibilities and integrate these into their core operations and business strategies. SR 2.0 is an approach diametrically opposed to models of SR that are characterised by short-term, bolt-on and one-size-fits-all approaches towards SR that use generic instruments and checklists to define an organisation's social responsibilities. SR 2.0 is about organisations constructing unique SR profiles. Building these interpretations, in our view (and recognised by ISO 26000), is an interactive exercise in which the organisation remains in continuous interaction with its stakeholders. Ambition about the role of business in society and the wish to leave a sustainable legacy are seen as a driver of social entrepreneurship.

interpretations of SR based on their own contexts, cultures and priorities. ISO 26000 acknowledges the organisation-specific character of SR by linking specific organisational characteristics on the one hand and the selection of SR priorities and identification of stakeholders on the other. Any organisation should use this as a starting point—the context of the organisation is supposed to guide formulating its unique SR profile.

Therefore, ambition is also central to SR 2.0—what would you want to achieve as an entrepreneur, director, employer or organisation? Or, in what way would organisations want to leave the world a better place than they found it? SR 2.0 does not only cover complying with what is expected of an organisation, for example, by guidelines, shareholders, governments or other stakeholders. As an organisation, you are encouraged to aspire to achieve something beyond the usual and go for it passionately—because of the morality behind the ideas. That is the signature note of SR 2.0 for modern organisations.

This is much more than being convinced of the business case for SR. As Al Gore puts it in his documentary *An Inconvenient Truth,* 'This isn't so much a political issues as it is a moral issue.' In SR 2.0 an inspiring and moral perspective takes centre stage. For example, social entrepreneurs, who have societal objectives at the heart of their business models, or companies that attempt to reduce or neutralise their carbon footprints.

A central starting point with SR 2.0 is that organisations define their engagement, based on their characteristics and context—they formulate an organisation-specific SR profile. ISO 26000 acknowledges this by stating in several passages that various aspects of guidance depend on the context in which the organisation operates and the key characteristics of the organisation.[12]

One of the central pillars of a SR profile is the SR impact areas of an organisation. Or, in other words: where the main ecological and social footprints lie. For a German company that trades textile products and that has outsourced its production activities to factories in Burma, this footprint is totally different than, for example, a banking corporation in Spain. Of course, several aspects of doing business can be identified that are similar for most organisations (such as energy usage in the office and CO_2 emissions from business travel), but the priorities within the SR profile of these two organisations are essentially almost completely different. These organisations are making impacts in different parts of the world and on different SR themes. Thus, the sustainability impact of these organisations cannot be compared. ISO 26000 acknowledges

12 The guideline states in this respect (ISO 2010: 69): 'To provide an informed basis for integrating social responsibility throughout the organisation, it is useful for the organisation to analyse how its key characteristics relate to social responsibility.'

this, as several passages in the guideline illustrate and which is expressed concisely and clearly in the part of the SR guideline in which indications are given for SR implementation.[13]

For the company in the textile business the most important sustainability impact probably lies with labour conditions and the potential use of child labour in the production facilities in Burma, with responsible use of the chemicals that are necessary to bleach and colour the textile, and with the CO_2 emissions that come from transportation of finished goods from Burma to the Netherlands.

For the banking group, the impacts are different. These are likely to be related to energy use, paper use, the CO_2 emissions of company cars and personal development in the workplace. The measure for SR within SR 2.0 is credibility: the more credibly an organisation accounts for its sustainability impacts, the greater the effects of its SR efforts.

Did you know...

To fly one person to Athens uses more energy than heating an average family home for an entire year.

Other characteristics of SR 2.0 include the deep integration of SR into the culture of an organisation, monitoring, measuring and improving initiatives and creating stakeholder engagement. SR is not only integrated in systems, structures and procedures—there is also wide support within the organisation and its organisational culture. Organisations do not want to be certified to standards because of the certificate, but because they appreciate the principles behind it and take those as a starting point of their actions. Greenwashing—making false or unjustified claims about their products, services or ambitions—is not an option: organisations know what their social responsibilities are, are ambitious regarding their social role and live and breathe their SR policies. Good examples of such companies are Seventh Generation and Triodos Bank.

A key element of SR 2.0 is monitoring, measuring and improvement. SR can been described as a 'moving target': it is a target that easily disappears from an organisation's radar if it does not keep an eye on it. In SR 2.0 an organisation monitors and measures its SR achievements and sets clear and ambitious goals to reduce its sustainability impacts and to contribute to society

Did you know...

MVO Nederland in 2008 reported that, according to environmental organisations, many car manufacturers and energy suppliers are guilty of greenwashing even though these manufacturers were able to make some solid claims and present evidence on their CSR performance.

---

13 'An organisation should conscientiously and methodically manage its own impacts [. . .]' (ISO 2010: 75).

to the largest extent possible. An organisation does not do that by itself, but in cooperation and discussion with stakeholders. By engaging in a continuous stakeholder dialogue, in which stakeholders are consulted in order to make their interests, demands, expectations and wishes part of the SR policy, the organisation can ensure its so-called 'license to operate' and its ability to innovate. All of these characteristics of SR 2.0 will be dealt with in this book.

3.5.1 The organisation-specific SR profile

ISO 26000 offers, by specifying SR core subjects, a basic set of SR themes which act as a *de minimis* to which any organisation should aspire. It further specifies a number of general SR principles (including respecting stakeholder interests) which should be the basis of any SR policy. The guideline's introduction illustrates this by stating that all core subjects are relevant for any organisation.[14]

A central characteristic of the new generation SR is thus that organisations give their own, organisation-specific, idiosyncratic meaning to SR. The so-called one-size-fits-all will no longer suffice, for two very good reasons: firstly, it makes an organisation's commitment towards SR untrustworthy; and, secondly, it simply does not work, since SR efforts are tagged on rather than embedded and so do not reflect an organisation's uniqueness. Therefore, any organisation must establish its own SR profile.

3.5.2 A SR profile: the ins and outs

The concept of an SR profile is referred to frequently in this book, but what exactly is it? An SR profile is the translation of the broad, all-encompassing and therefore diffuse concept that SR is to an organisation-specific context. To do this, the organisation must have a clear vision and ambition about SR, an organisation-specific perception of SR, a clear view of its priorities, an understanding of the current situation and a concrete plan for how strategies can be implemented in existing policies. The SR profile is relevant for public, private and social organisations of any size and from any sector. Indeed, even a single-person company or a societal organisation with five employees can

---

14 Furthermore, in an explanation about the applicability of ISO 26000 for SMEs, it is stated that organisations should be aware (ISO 2010: 8): '[t]hat when reviewing all seven core subjects and identifying the relevant issues, the organisation's own context, conditions, resources and stakeholder interests should be taken into account, recognising that all core subjects, but not all issues will be relevant for every organisation'.

engage in SR in their own ways. Consequently, it is every individual organisation's responsibility to develop its organisation-specific SR profile, which is also acknowledged by ISO 26000.[15]

The process of arriving at a definition of SR can be seen as a process of sense-making—formulating an organisation-specific meaning often provides a lot of clarity about the 'why, what and how' of SR. By making the SR concept organisation-specific it becomes relevant and recognisable for all employees and stakeholders, and enables the question 'What does SR mean or comprise for our organisation?' to be answered. In this process the ideas and opinions of different stakeholders and, especially, employees have to be taken into account and, hopefully, connect with the current SR activities that have already been undertaken by the organisation. SR is not something new for every organisation—certain activities fall under the SR umbrella. Often organisations take a stance regarding the 3Ps and the relationships between them. Do policies on people and planet contribute to profit? Or is profit a requirement to be able to engage with people and planet? Or is the specific characteristic of SR for the organisation that a 'fourth P' is used: for example, partnership, pleasure, pride or prestige? When the organisation has an overview of what SR exactly entails for the organisation and how this relates to core processes and activities, the next step is to explicitly draw up the future vision, ambition and priorities of the organisation in relation to SR.

3.5.2.1 Vision, ambition and priorities

Vision and ambition guide an organisation. Having a vision for SR is essential for organisations to translate the relevance of the organisation-specific concept for employees and stakeholders—SR is guided in a certain direction. This clarifies how SR is elaborated at a strategic level—which SR route should we take and why? As a part of this vision, the ambition for SR has to be made explicit. What do we want to achieve? What are we striving for? With a clear vision, ambition and motivations, an organisation gives SR an organisation-specific direction. Of course, this has to be consistent with its general vision, ambition, strategy and policies. This process is a fine-tuning of the organisation-specific meaning of SR. Therefore, the organisation has to be aware of the type of culture it has, its attitude towards SR, the opportunities and threats, and the expectations and demands of its stakeholders and society in general.

---

15 '[I]t is an individual organisation's responsibility to identify what is relevant and significant for the organisation to address, through its own considerations and through dialogue with stakeholders' (ISO 2010: vi).

Following the vision, a SR profile contains the SR priorities for the organisation. The meaning, ambition and vision determine the context and direction of the SR initiative, the SR priorities and concrete contents (e.g. SR activities). A characteristic of an effective SR policy is that clear choices have been made. There are a number of good reasons for this, such as the fact that the resources an organisation is able to invest in SR are not unlimited. Furthermore, the visibility and recognisability of SR inside and outside the organisation, and the development of a unique SR profile, require clear choices. Chapter 7 discusses how to determine these priorities and elaborates the possible criteria that can be used by an organisation for doing this. Two essential elements in this are the sustainability impact (what is our most important social and ecological footprint?) and influence (to what degree are we able to influence our footprints?). These two aspects are not supposed to be dealt with in an isolated manner, but in consultation with stakeholders.[16]

Thinking in terms of impact and influence is also about the business case of SR—what exactly is the value of SR for our organisation? Where can we make a profit out of SR? This can manifest itself in reducing costs and increasing revenues, but also in increasing intangibles. Examples of this are differentiating the organisation in the market it operates in, improving customer relations, reducing absenteeism, developing competence through employee volunteering, attracting and retaining talented employees and specialists, and improving the image and the reputation of an organisation. Prioritising also gives the SR initiative a character unique to the organisation enabling employees to better identify themselves with SR and the organisation—certainly when they can contribute to the SR initiative themselves. This uniqueness can be shaped at both the organisational and the departmental level. In the latter case, there still needs to be an organisation-wide SR umbrella in which departmental SR initiatives fit, but it does have its own accents. Moreover, a focus on impact and influence implies that the organisation is able to communicate a clear and credible message towards its stakeholders. Finally, it is important that the priorities within the SR profile are well balanced, with attention to the 3Ps (people, planet, profits). Practice shows that environmental aspects especially tend to receive a good deal of attention in many organisations, since these often provide the most tangible results. This means that the 'white

---

16 'Although an organisation itself may believe it understands societal expectations of its social responsibility, it should nevertheless consider involving stakeholders in the identification process to broaden the perspective on the core subjects and issues' (ISO 2010: 71).

spots' or underexposed aspects of SR have to be given greater priority in order to achieve a well-balanced SR profile.

3.5.2.2 Gap analysis

Stakeholders are not only interested in the direction of the organisation when talking about SR. The current situation—Where does the organisation come from? What is the organisation's starting point?—is also important. Without an idea of the 'zero-situation' it is impossible to have a view on possible improvements or relevant additions to the current SR activities. However, to evaluate all possible activities in the field of SR that the organisation can undertake, is not useful either. To focus on the priorities set by the organisation itself, a gap analysis or diagnosis can efficiently be executed. The SR priorities are, after all, themes or subjects on which the organisation wants to focus, on which the stakeholders expect initiatives, and where the impact and influence of the organisation lies. Moreover, mapping the current situation offers an organisation the possibility to inform its stakeholders about the kind of activities it already undertakes to enhance its positive sustainability impacts, and to reduce its negative ones. Of course, the gap analysis offers insights about where extra SR efforts are necessary to realise the organisation's ambition and goals. These additional SR efforts are reflected in the action plan. Where the diagnosis is specifically directed towards the priorities, this also goes for the action plan: the identified gaps from the gap analysis have to be filled in. The action plan clarifies what the organisation will do, when it will do it and what the organisational consequences will be. With this, the action plan gives an overview of the way the organisation chooses and the pace at which it will realise its SR initiative. ISO 26000 also acknowledges that realistic planning and expectations are important in this respect—SR doesn't happen overnight, nor will all parts of the organisation be in sync when implementing it.[17]

The action plan links the organisation's meaning, vision and ambition with existing organisational structures and systems, such as quality management instruments (for example, ISO 9001), the planning and control cycle, departmental plans and/or existing programmes. In addition, determining responsibilities and timescales is part of the action plan. An effective SR policy

---

17 'It is also important to recognise that the process of integrating social responsibility throughout an organisation does not occur all at once or at the same pace for all core subjects and issues. It may be helpful to develop a plan for addressing some social responsibility issues in the short term and some over a longer period of time' (ISO 2010: 75).

requires a robust connection between strategy ('guiding') and implementation ('organising').

3.5.2.3 Communication and support

For organisations that are serious about SR, the development of a SR profile is, on the one hand, an ideal way to translate the concept into organisational language while, on the other, to develop a clear vision which an organisation can work with in the coming years. Organisations that have been working with SR for years can use the ideas and starting points behind a SR profile to evaluate their SR strategies and ,where necessary, to 'reboot' in order to operate according to ISO 26000's line of thought.

Besides 'guiding' and 'organising', a SR profile offers a clear framework for communication, clarifying how the organisation sees SR, why it wants to be socially responsible, what it is going to do and what it hopes to achieve. An organisation can choose what information from its SR profile it wants to disclose, so that stakeholders receive the information they want and need. This information can vary from an ambition (what does the organisation want to achieve and when?) to concrete results (how did the organisation perform in relation to last year's targets?).

An important test of any effective SR profile is the degree to which the policy is supported within the organisation. If there is little or no internal support then SR will have little external value either. Worse still, an organisation may run the risk of stakeholders perceiving that it is engaging in an SR initiative that is not very credible or is a form of greenwashing. Creating support is a central part of the integration of SR within an organisation.[18]

For this reason an organisation can never start too early to garner support for a SR initiative. The commitment of top management is essential, as is offering context and developing knowledge. When employees cannot place the SR initiative in a larger context ('Where on earth does this come from?') or have no knowledge about its contents ('What is this about? I don't think this has anything to do with my work, does it?'), the initiative is bound to fail at the start. Therefore, in order to create support, knowledge development and communication are essential. An additional advantage of knowledge development is that every employee involved in the process (for example, by participating

18 ISO 26000 formulates it as follows (ISO 2010: 74): 'Building social responsibility into every aspect of an organisation involves commitment and understanding at all levels of the organisation. In the early stages of an organisation's efforts related to social responsibility, the focus of awareness building should be on increasing understanding of the aspects of social responsibility [. . .].'

in a working group) is better able to contribute to the SR initiative from his or her field of expertise. Furthermore, there are a number of instruments and measures available for organisations to work on creating support, such as increasing employee involvement by:

- Asking for ideas and suggestions

- Creating a well-balanced working group (consisting of employees from several departments and functions)

- Making the SR initiative visible (for example, by organising one or a few concrete SR projects or events)

- Identifying quick wins to realise achievements in the short term

- Creating symbols (for example SR ambassadors)

- Connecting SR to existing initiatives (for example, spontaneous SR-related actions of employees)

- Acknowledging earlier efforts as concrete examples of SR

- Consulting employees about the SR ambition the organisation has set

- Continuing communication about SR (using existing media, such as newsletters, meetings and speeches)

- Making SR part of departmental plans and connecting it with organisational goals

Chapters 7 and 8 discuss the selection of SR priorities and SR implementation in detail. These chapters provide additional information about integrating SR, methods to do so and ISO 26000's suggestions for this.

3.6 Structure of the guideline: the contents of ISO 26000 in a nutshell

ISO 26000 consists of seven clauses, two annexes and a bibliography. The core of the SR guideline consists of the generic SR principles (Clause 4), recognising and acknowledging social responsibilities and stakeholder engagement (Clause 5), the SR core subjects and SR issues (Clause 6) and the integration of SR in an organisation (Clause 7). These are preceded by the scope of the guideline (Clause 1), the terms and definitions used in the guideline (Clause

2) and an elaboration on SR and how this concept is interpreted by the guideline (Clause 3).

Although this seems like a clear-cut setup of the guideline, not all subjects are structured by ISO 26000 in a clear way—it seems as though, at some points, the guideline is 'searching for the right way'. The concept of 'sphere of influence' is an example of this. The guideline mentions this in a paragraph within the section that deals with recognising social responsibilities and stakeholder engagement, but also elaborates on this within the section that deals with implementation and integration of SR.

3.6.1 Clauses in ISO 26000

The four most important clauses in ISO 26000 are preceded by a clarification of the scope of the guideline. This explains the contents of ISO 26000, that ISO 26000 is applicable to all types of organisations and the purpose of ISO 26000. Furthermore, it specifically states that ISO 26000 is not meant as a standard for a management system or for certification purposes.

Next, the most important terms and definitions that are used in ISO 26000 are described ('Terms, definitions and abbreviated terms'). This glossary contains the definitions of the most important concepts used in the guideline, such as due diligence, organisational impact, sphere of influence and vulnerable group.

The definitions that are described in the guideline are actually pretty obvious—there are no strange, new or unexpected terms or definitions. At best (or worst), the text mentions some typical terms and phrases that seem better suited for large multinationals with significant social and environmental impacts than to other types of organisation. An example of this is the use of the concept of 'indigenous people', which is often used in the context of companies with overseas production facilities or extractive industries.

After the terms and definitions ISO 26000 directs attention to the background of SR. Clause 3 includes a description of trends and developments, characteristics of SR and the relationship between SR and sustainable development. Moreover, this clause pays attention to the relationship between ISO 26000 and the responsibilities of governments in SR. It notes, for example, that ISO 26000 does not offer starting points for

Did you know...

The diversity barometer of consultancy GITP from 2008 indicates that 83% of companies in Zuid-Limburg, a southern province of the Netherlands, perceive a cultural diversity policy as unnecessary. For all Dutch companies this percentage is 59%. Interestingly, of all companies that find such a diversity policy necessary, only one-third put their principles into practice.

governments to decide which SR subjects should be included in laws and rules. In addition, it states that governments, just like any other kind of organisation, can use the guideline to formulate their own internal SR policies. The guideline also points at the role of government in stimulating SR among companies, but offers no further specific guidance on this issue.

Next, the general SR principles on which ISO 26000 is based are described. These principles form starting points or foundations for any SR policy. They are:

1. Accountability

2. Transparency

3. Ethical behaviour

4. Respect for stakeholder interests

5. Respect for the rule of law

6. Respect for international norms of behaviour

7. Respect for human rights

Organisations that implement ISO 26000 should, at the very least, apply these principles. It is optional for organisations to apply additional principles. Chapter 4 puts forward several suggestions for additional principles on which an organisation can found its SR policy (and which are actually also part of ISO 26000, but are not explicitly named as general SR principles).

Clause 5 exhibits two basic practices of SR-recognising social responsibilities and the relevance of SR and stakeholder engagement. In this part, the guideline pays attention to the relationships between organisations, stakeholders and society as a whole, the identification of an organisation's stakeholders and their interests, and the role of the organisation's sphere of influence in SR. Clause 5 also introduces the guideline's core subjects.

Did you know...

In a survey among Romanian companies, researchers found that nearly two-thirds of these were not familiar with the concept of CSR, leading these researchers to conclude that the position of Romanian society is way behind other European and even international ones.[19]

Next, the seven SR core subjects are elaborately described in Clause 6, as follows:

---

19 Source: Mihalache and Stremţan 2010.

1. Organisational governance

2. Human rights

3. Labour practices

4. The environment

5. Fair operating practices

6. Consumer issues

7. Community involvement and development

Every SR core subject is accompanied by an explanation of the contents, the subject, the scope and the grounding principles. In addition, the text includes considerations around the core subjects and specifies the related actions and expectations of organisations. The specification of the related actions and expectations is done per SR issue. With the exception of 'Organisational governance', all core subjects comprise a number of SR issues.

The final clause, Clause 7, deals with the integration of SR throughout the organisation. This part of ISO 26000 essentially consists of recommendations about SR implementation. Topics that are discussed in this part include communicating about SR, enhancing the credibility of SR claims, and reviewing and improving SR initiatives and actions of the organisation.

3.6.2 Annexes in ISO 26000

The first annex (Annex A) of ISO 26000 provides an overview of existing voluntary SR-related initiatives and instruments, divided into two extensive tables. The first table gives an overview of initiatives and instruments that are applicable to every sector while the second consists of sector-specific initiatives and instruments. The tables list the SR core subjects related to each of the initiatives and instruments and which specifications regarding the integration of SR they cover.

ISO 26000 ends with a list of abbreviations and a bibliography, in which, among others, different international guidelines, standards, conventions and treaties referred to in the text can be found.

Misuse of ISO 26000

Due to the prefix 'ISO' it is very tempting to refer to ISO 26000 as a certifiable standard or to develop and offer a new standard that is 'based on ISO 26000'. The guideline clearly states, however, that it is not meant for certification or contractual use (ISO 2010: 1). To alert users to potential misuse, six kinds of potential misuse of the standard have been identified.[a]

1. Misleading representation: for instance, listing ISO 26000 on a website under the heading 'certification'

2. Use in contracts: under no circumstance should ISO 26000 be used in contracts

3. Use in public procurement: governments should not mention ISO 26000 in procurement to avoid the implication that suppliers are obliged to meet the requirements contained in ISO 26000

4. Use in regulation and/or legislation: as ISO 26000 does not specify any requirements, merely recommendations, it is impossible to use for, and is not meant for, regulatory use

5. Use for certification: this point has been made throughout this book and is stressed in the guideline and by most standardisation institutes

6. Use as reference in certifiable social responsibility standards: although this is not what ISO 26000 is intended for, this does not mean that organisations have refrained from using ISO 26000 in this way. However, not every standardisation organisation respects this statement, as shown by the development of DS 26001 in Denmark.[b]

Once an organisation or person falls foul of a particular kind of misuse, there are a few recommended actions. These recommendations include pointing out to the originator of the message what ISO 26000 is and what it is not meant to be. Furthermore, when an organisation is asked to provide ISO 26000 certification it should advise the originator how to properly use ISO 2600 and demonstrate this.

Although these suggestions are commendable, and it is clear that ISO 26000 cannot be used for certification in its current form, we expect that, eventually, an international ISO 26000 certification, in one form or another, will emerge. We would largely ascribe such a development to the desire of companies to show their relevant stakeholders that they manage SR in a structured way.

a www.26k-estimation.com/html/misuse_of_iso_26000.html, accessed 26 March 2011.
b webshop.ds.dk/product/M243304/ds-260012010.aspx, accessed 26 March 2011.

3.7 **Final words**

As well as the reasons for developing ISO 26000, this chapter discussed what type of standard ISO 26000 is, how it differs from other standards, and what its functions and aims are. From this it becomes clear that ISO 26000 is an ambitious guideline that can provide structure and guidance in the jungle of SR standards. The chapter also noted that, with the development of ISO 26000, a different light is shed on the claim that no standard can lead on SR. ISO 26000 acknowledges the uniqueness of organisations in determining social responsibilities, offers room for own interpretations and encourages the formulation of an organisation-specific SR profile. Leipziger's analogy of SR being a journey still stands (Leipziger 2003): social responsibilities change, just as do organisational ambitions, stakeholder interests and society's expectations regarding the behaviour of organisations.

'Taking ISO 26000 literally' should always be accompanied by 'within the spirit of' and the organisation that wants to work according to any kind of standard should do this in an organisation-specific way. ISO 26000 perfectly suits this view and, furthermore, guides the idea of SR 2.0—a new generation of SR whereby the unique SR profile of an organisation is based on its characteristics and on the key aspects of: ambitions that reach further than the business case for SR; a new morality; the deep integration of SR; and the creation of stakeholder engagement. This chapter described what an organisation-specific SR profile consists of and what process an organisation should go through in order to formulate such a profile.

Even though SR warrants an organisation-specific interpretation, there is still a number of basic general SR principles. These principles are central in the next chapter and form the first of the four 'core clauses' in the outline of ISO 26000.

Interlude II
Myths and misunderstandings about ISO 26000: Part 1

II.1 **Introduction**

Throughout the long development of ISO 26000, right up to its publication on 1 November 2010, the guideline has raised as many questions as answers. Often it is not (totally) clear what ISO 26000 exactly is and what the guideline aims for. Several myths and misunderstandings have already come into existence. In this Interlude (the first of two on this large topic) three of these myths and misunderstandings surrounding ISO 26000 will be considered and clarified. These are:

- ISO 26000 is a management system standard

- ISO 26000 is meant to be used only by (large) companies

- ISO 26000 is about the content of SR and not about SR implementation

The explanations accompanying these myths and misunderstandings provide extra clarity about the objectives, starting points and background of ISO 26000.

II.2 **ISO 26000 is a management system standard**

ISO 26000 is a guideline for SR. A guideline can be classified as a so-called International Standard, of which ISO has developed over 17,500 on a range of topics and continues to develop more annually. As a guideline ISO 26000 provides organisations with advice on SR, especially on the process of defining the social responsibilities of organisations and implementing them.[1] Hence, it is an objective of the guideline to help organisations contribute to sustainable development.

ISO 26000 is not a management system standard, which can be defined as an organisational structure and coherent set of agreements and ways of working for the systematic control and improvement of organisational processes in order to realise certain predetermined objectives. The SR guideline is therefore different to, for example, ISO 9001 and ISO 14001, the well-known management system standards for quality and environmental management. ISO 26000 does contain a number of ingredients for a SR management system, however, and organisations that have decided to work to ISO 26000 (especially those that already have a management system in place) will probably encounter relatively few problems in developing a SR management system inspired by ISO 26000. There have been several attempts to develop a SR management system (or to describe one) and there are companies that have developed their own versions. However, these are not internationally recognised nor authoritative and do not have the potential to become influential and widespread to the degree that an ISO 26000-based SR management system would. However, ISO has not developed and does not propose establishing a management system for ISO 26000.

Neither does ISO 26000 replace current management systems such as ISO 9001, ISO 14001, OHSAS 18001 (occupational health and safety) and ISO 27001 (information security and privacy), nor does it replace standards and guidelines such as SA8000 (working conditions in the supply chain), AA1000SES (stakeholder engagement) and GRI (sustainability reporting). The guideline is intended to be used as a framework for SR, integrating existing norms and standards with developed, developing or yet-to-be-developed organisational initiatives, programmes and strategies.. Where there is a similarity, it is that

---

1 'This International Standard provides guidance on the underlying principles of social responsibility, recognizing social responsibility and engaging stakeholders, the core subjects and issues pertaining to social responsibility and on ways to integrate socially responsible behaviour into the organization' (ISO 2010: vi).

ISO 26000 emphasises the importance of improvements in the performance of organisations.

So, ISO 26000 is a guideline that advises and supports the SR efforts of organisations. It does not prescribe or formulate requirements—but rather suggests ways in which SR can be organised and aligned with existing management systems.

II.3 **ISO 26000 only applies to (large) companies**

ISO 26000 is meant for all types of organisation, irrespective of size, sector, location and market in which they operate. This means that ISO 26000 is applicable to companies of any size, as well as to governments, NGOs, educational institutions, museums, volunteer organisations, churches, sectoral organisations and (virtual) network organisations. This one-size-fits-all approach partly stems from the multi-stakeholder group of experts involved in drafting the guideline. But can it work in practice?

A study into the relevance of ISO 26000 for SMEs conducted by the IISD (International Institute for Sustainable Development) (Perera 2008), which looked at both developed and developing countries and consulted with SME advisors and support organisations, concluded that the guideline is going to be difficult for small businesses to work with (see also Interlude V). The entire consultation process behind ISO 26000 has been characterised by a lack of participation of individual SMEs (though organisations representing SMEs did participate in the process). Elsewhere in this book it is noted that both the language used and the selection of core SR subjects and issues in ISO 26000 seem particularly slanted towards large, internationally operating enterprises that (can) cause considerable environmental or social damage. Other potential users of the guideline could well be put off by this. However, the guideline evidently includes actions, references, definitions and concepts that are specific for non-multinational organisations or that are at least more easily applicable to other kinds of organisations.

Box II.1 explains the ways in which ISO 26000 can relate to, and be applicable for, SMEs.

Box II.1 **ISO 26000 for SMEs**

SMEs have the same potential as any other organisation to conduct business in a socially responsible way. ISO 26000 acknowledges the differences between companies of different sizes and makes some relevant remarks about that. For example, internal management procedures, reporting to stakeholders, and other processes, can be more flexible and informal for SMEs than for large enterprises, under the condition that appropriate levels of transparency are maintained.

Also, SMEs should encourage governments, collective organisations (such as industry bodies and professional organisations) and national standardisation bodies to help them with SR. One way this can be done is by developing practical guides and programmes about applying ISO 26000. Moreover, SMEs should preferably work together with such organisations in order to use available resources more efficiently and undertake action in a more focused way. For example, stakeholder identification for comparable companies from the same sector can sometimes be better dealt with collectively.

Larger organisations with more resources and experience in the field of SR could consider supporting SMEs by raising awareness, sharing experiences and drawing good examples to their attention. A good example of this is the industry programme, the regional programme and the SR champions programme of MVO Nederland, the Dutch 'knowledge centre' for SR. In these programmes, instruments and initiatives are developed to bring SR to the attention of companies, sharing knowledge and experiences in the field of SR both with participants of these programmes and with other companies.

It is also important to mention here that an essential aspect of SR for organisations such as governments and sector organisations is not dealt with at all in ISO 26000. Developing and deploying policies aimed at stimulating SR among organisations at the local, regional or national level is, we feel, a very notable omission. Such organisations have a key role in specifying social responsibilities based on a particular sector or organisation's environmental and social effects and translating this into both policy development and operationalisation.

When the guideline refers to policy, it predominantly refers to an organisation's strategy and the policies an organisation has developed in order to reduce the negative effects of its operations (also in relation to governmental organisations). It does not deal with governmental policy or the policies of sector organisations that are aimed at stimulating SR among enterprises and member organisations. The guideline does, however, emphasise using the influence of an organisation to improve socially responsible behaviour.[2]

So, we may conclude that, as currently formulated, ISO 26000 appears to be mainly applicable to companies. Is this problematic? Well, from the perspective of the roles and responsibilities of business in sustainable development, there are good reasons for such a focus. Looking at the room for manoeuvre offered in ISO 26000 (the fact that the guideline encourages (potential) users of the guideline to interpret SR in a way that is congruent with the specific characteristics of their organisation), it can be said that ISO 26000 is equally applicable to SMEs and other types of organisations. This is reflected in the guideline.[3]

II.4 **The scope of ISO 26000 is limited to the content of SR**

ISO 26000 deals with both the content of SR and the process of SR implementation—both the 'what' and the 'how' of SR. On the one hand, the guideline defines essential SR concepts, tries to create uniformity in SR terminology, offers departure points for SR policies, and offers guidelines to recognise and prioritise the social responsibilities of organisations. On the other hand, it deals with SR implementation and the process of integrating SR within organisations.

The content of SR is mainly reflected in the identification of SR core subjects and SR issues. The SR core subjects are, according to the guideline, the pillars of SR and, to a certain extent, relevant for any organisation. The SR issues specified as sub-items for each SR core subject are, on the other hand,

---

2 'In addition to being responsible for its own decisions and activities, an organization may, in some situations, have the ability to affect the behaviour of organizations/parties with which it has relationships. Such situations are considered to fall within an organization's sphere of influence' (ISO 2010: 16).

3 'This International Standard is intended to be useful to all types of organisations in the private, public and non-profit sectors, whether large or small, and whether operating in developed or developing countries. While not all parts of this International Standard will be of equal use to all types of organisations, all core subjects are relevant to every organisation. All core subjects comprise a number of issues, and it is an individual organization's responsibility to identify which issues are relevant and significant for the organization to address, through its own considerations and through dialogue with stakeholders' (ISO 2010: vi).

not relevant for all organisations. This is regularly emphasised throughout the guideline.

The final chapter of ISO 26000 deals with SR implementation. Processes such as creating stakeholder engagement, increasing the credibility of the SR initiative of an organisation and communicating about SR are highlighted. The guideline also discusses how to determine SR priorities based on the sustainability impact of an organisation. The process of stakeholder engagement is dealt with in more detail earlier on in the guideline, as this is essential for the content of a successful SR policy as well.

4

SR principles

4.1 **Introduction**

In the previous chapters attention has been paid to several principles and starting points of (C)SR. For example, Chapter 2 showed that CSR has to do with both the concepts of responsibility and accountability. These aspects of CSR can be seen as its two fundamental notions or perhaps principles. ISO 26000 formulates seven generic SR principles—these principles take centre stage in this chapter.

Firstly, it is explained what principles are and what purpose they serve. This is illustrated with several real-life examples that show in what way these principles manifest themselves within organisations. Secondly, attention is directed towards the different kinds of principles that are used within ISO 26000. A distinction is made between the general SR principles and the principles that underlie the SR core subjects. After that, the general SR principles of ISO 26000 are briefly described and explained. Also, a number of additional principles are discussed that are not explicitly named as general SR principles within the ISO 26000 guideline, but which could well have been. Finally, the SR principles are dealt with more elaborately and the expectations towards organisations according to these principles discussed.

4.2 **Principles as starting points**

The word 'principle' is often used in all kind of conversations—but what exactly is a principle? Wikipedia defines a principle as 'a comprehensive and fundamental law, doctrine or assumption. It can be a rule or code of conduct. It can be a law or fact of nature underlying the working of an artificial device'. The description of a principle as some kind of code of conduct, rule or norm for behaviour is the most appropriate in the context of SR. Principles can be seen as orientation points for organisations (or for individuals within an organisation) to guide actions, to aspire to internal consistency and to discipline behaviour. A principle can be seen as a cornerstone for decision-making or behaviour.

So principles are guidelines or starting points, often with a moral dimension, for organisations. By communicating these principles organisations give a signal and clarify their position: 'this is what our organisation stands for' or 'this is important to our organisation'. In that sense, principles also fulfil a function as a test or standard: an organisation can evaluate its behaviour by means of the principles and determine whether or not its behaves in accordance with them.

Many NGOs, company associations that stimulate and promote SR and sustainable development, sectoral organisations and individual companies have formulated SR principles. One of the more well-known examples are the principles for companies formulated by the Caux Round Table (CRT), an international network of companies that extols the virtues of moral capitalism. These 'ethical norms for acceptable businesses behaviour', as the CRT calls them, were formulated as early as 1994 and deal with, among other things, an organisation's contribution to economic development, social development, environmental development and the support of responsible globalisation. A responsible company, according to the CRT principles, supports open and honest multilateral trade as a participant in the global marketplace. Moreover, a responsible company is not involved in corruption, bribery, money laundering or any other illegal activities.[1] Another example of SR principles are the Global Sullivan Principles of Social Responsibility. These principles form a voluntary code of conduct for companies and are meant as 'a catalyst and compass for corporate responsibility and accountability. [. . .] The Global Sullivan Principles advance a development framework that enables businesses of all sizes and in all sectors to pursue their business objectives while being mindful and respectful of employees and the communities in which

---

1 www.cauxroundtable.org.

they operate'.[2] Companies that work according to these principles commit themselves, among other things, to respect the freedom of association for employees and offer equal opportunities to employees at every level, irrespective of issues such as gender, disability, skin colour, race, age and sexual orientation.

The Global Compact of the UN can also be seen as a set of principles with which companies can voluntarily comply.[3] The Global Compact specifies ten principles in the field of human rights, labour, environment and anti-corruption, among which it proposes the abolition of child labour and the use of the precautionary principle concerning environmental issues. A final example of a well-known set of principles are the guidelines of the OECD. These multilaterally developed guidelines contain general principles and recommendations for companies to improve responsible and sustainable behaviour. They deal with the areas of workers' rights, consumer interests, competition, and science and technology. The OECD guidelines clarify what governments expect in the field of socially responsible business from their nation's companies that operate abroad. They also offer guidance in developing company codes of conduct in order to deal with social and community issues such as child labour, environment and corruption. So far, 41 national governments, including 11 countries that are not members of the OECD, have signed the guidelines.

Many individual companies have also formulated CSR principles, for example in the form of a code of conduct (see Box 4.1 for an example).

Did you know...

Several multinationals in the Netherlands acknowledge the problem of the 'pink ceiling' — the fact that gay people experience barriers reaching the higher echelons of companies, according to the magazine *Management Team*.

2 www.thesullivanfoundation.org.
3 An interesting fact is that, in June 2009, Georg Kell, executive director of the Global Compact within the UN, asked the secretary general of ISO to remove Global Compact from the annex of ISO 26000. The reason for this was that the Global Compact was disappointed that 'neither in the body of the standard nor in the annex is there any recognition of the world's foremost social responsibility initiative'. Both organisations have since then publicly emphasised the complementary nature of the initiatives.

Box 4.1 ING's 'business principles'

Source: www.ing.com/cms/idc_cgi_isapi.dll?IdcService=GET_FILE&dDocName=407888_EN&RevisionSelecti onMethod=latestReleased, accessed 17 April 2011

- We act with **integrity**
- We are **open and clear**
- We **respect** each other
- We are socially and environmentally **responsible**

Around 40% of the world's multinationals have used the OECD guidelines as a basis for their own commitments. The first 'business principles' of Shell date back to 1976 and have been revised on numerous occasions since then. Although Shell has recently been deleted from the Dow Jones Sustainability Index, it has a policy stating that it wants to be a good neighbour for all local communities. These principles are presented to all contractors and suppliers of Shell, before they sign a contract. After that, the principles become part of the contract and Shell is known to monitor compliance. Another example is Hydro,[4] (formerly Norsk Hydro). The company uses the following basic principles:

- **Respect for human rights**. Hydro supports the principles set forth in the Universal Declaration of Human Rights. We shall make sure that our operations are conducted in accordance with basic human rights standards.

- **Contributing to sustainability**. Through developing profitable business and active engagement with local communities, we aim to ensure that our business practices contribute to long-term economic and social development. We will work with government and civil society to define roles and responsibilities for social development.

- **Diversity**. Hydro will not discriminate on the basis of gender, religion, race, national or ethnic origin, cultural background, social group, disability, sexual orientation, marital status, age or political opinion. We recognise the intrinsic value of the different cultures in which we operate, and will show respect for these cultures in all our business practices. Hydro will pay special attention to the rights,

4 www.hydro.com.

requirements and cultural integrity of indigenous people affected by our operations.

- **Dialogue**. To ensure that our activities are properly adapted to meet local conditions and generate positive benefits both for the company and the community, we are prepared to enter into an open dialogue with relevant stakeholders. We shall give attention to initiatives and input which serve to improve our social responsibility standards and practices.

- **Integrity**. Hydro shall maintain high standards of integrity. This means that we shall be honest and fair in all our dealings. We shall not permit or tolerate engagement in bribery or other forms of corruption.

ECORYS,[5] a research and consultancy organisation, has committed itself to its own set of principles, which includes compliance with laws and rules, stakeholder engagement, CSR implementation and communication about CSR performance.

The CSR principles of the Spanish company Gamesa,[6] active in the field of sustainable energy solutions, are formulated in a code of conduct and include promises with respect to the promotion of training, avoiding discrimination, supporting research into technologies that respect the environment and testing if suppliers comply to their own CSR criteria. The code of conduct functions as a 'formal expression of the values and good practices that will guide Gamesa's conduct and that of all personnel subject to this code of conduct when carrying out its responsibilities and functions. The code is a statement of the company's willingness to comply with good business ethics and will act as a document for consultation in cases of conflict of interests'. Finally, the CSR principles of Singapore-based BCD Travel[7] encompass four areas, including the health and safety of its employees as well as the privacy and protection of personal data from customers.

Today, a majority of companies have formulated their own CSR principles, whether as a part of a formal code of conduct or as part of their mission statement. A study by the ILO (Edwards *et al.* 2007) shows that most British multinationals had a code of conduct which contained attention to CSR. In practice, most codes of conduct appear to include topics such as integrity in relationships with subcontractors, the use of company properties and compliance

---

5 www.ecorys.nl.
6 www.gamesacorp.com.
7 www.bcdtravel.sg.

with laws and rules, according to a study conducted in 2008 by Axentis and the Open Compliance and Ethics Group. SR principles in general form a pillar or starting point for the SR policy of organisations and can also be seen as a form of self-regulation.

4.3 General SR principles and principles of SR core subjects

ISO 26000 emphasises morality and takes a view on the equity of standards, guidelines and behavioural rules, but also states that this depends on the specific context of an organisation.

However, within ISO 26000 the following general SR principles are mentioned:

- Accountability

- Transparency

- Ethical behaviour

- Respect for stakeholder interests

- Respect for the rule of law

- Respect for international norms of behaviour

- Respect for human rights

ISO 26000 acknowledges that no exhaustive list of SR principles can be compiled. Therefore, these general principles serve as some sort of minimum conditions: any organisation should at least apply these seven SR principles. It is striking to note that a number of principles, which according to some would be classified as inherent to SR and sustainable development, are missing from the list. An example relates to the notion of 'intergenerational' since that is an integral part of most definitions of sustainable development.[8] The

---

8 'Sustainable development is about meeting the needs of society while living within the planet's ecological limits and without jeopardising the ability of future generations to meet their needs. Sustainable development has three dimensions—economic, social and environmental—which are interdependent; for instance, the elimination of poverty requires the promotion of social justice and economic development, and the protection of the environment' (ISO 2010: 9).

principle could then perhaps be formulated as 'respect for the interests of future generations' or 'stewardship'.

Another example deals with the concept of impact or, better, sustainability impact. Any organisation has its own ecological and social footprint. This means that the overall picture of the so-called external effects that organisations cause, differ per organisation.[9] The specific sustainability impact of an organisation should be guiding its SR efforts (see Chapter 7 for details on the selection of SR priorities). Furthermore, there are aspects of these footprints that are typical for organisations and that differ from the footprints of other entities, such as individuals. Consequently this principle could be formulated as 'sustainability impact of the organisation'. A third example is the idea of continuous improvement. Even though striving for improvement of SR performance is referred to in several parts of

Did you know...

2007 data from the Ecological Footprint Atlas compiled by the Global Footprint Network published in October 2010 shows that the ecological footprint in 2006 was 2.7 global hectares per person, while the world average biocapacity was 1.8 global hectares per person. In 1961, the footprint was about half of what Earth could supply.

the ISO 26000 guideline (it is, for example, a frequently recurring item within the related actions and expectations that are specified by ISO 26000 for nearly all SR issues), it is not formulated as a SR principle. A reason for this may be that continuous improvement as a principle is perceived as being too general and too unspecific in the light of formulating the social responsibilities of organisations. However, SR has no end—and ISO 26000 acknowledges this. The societal responsibilities of organisations change overtime, for example, because the *zeitgeist* is changing, but also because other concrete demands and interests play a role with an organisation's stakeholders.[10]

It is especially strange that the principles in the first two examples are not mentioned within ISO 26000, since the SR guideline points out the importance

---

9   This footprint is partly the same, or is at least comparable, for all organisations. For example, many service companies have a physical office location and their employees transport themselves by car to their clients, which causes a certain amount of CO_2 emissions. Moreover, certain organisations have to deal with SR-related topics such as the percentage of women in management positions and ergonomic office design. This comparability increases when the organisations are more homogenous (size, activities, sector, geographic location).

10 'Recognising social responsibility is a continuous process. [. . .] Ongoing activities should be reviewed as necessary so that the organisation can be confident that its social responsibility is still being addressed and can determine whether additional issues need to be taken into account' (ISO 2010: 16).

of taking care of, and of not undermining, future generations' interests and, in addition, since the document is saturated with the concept of impact.

The first two examples are also generally accepted as important principles within sustainable development and SR. The third example is a general starting point for, for example, ISO management system standards and many other management systems and models. Although these three principles are not fully covered by the seven principles of ISO 26000, organisations can still take these principles, just like other relevant principles, as additional foundations for their SR policy. This is fully in line with ISO 26000.

4.3.1 Principles for SR core subjects

In addition to the general SR principles there is a second category of principles to be found in ISO 26000. These are principles that underlie the different SR core subjects which are central to the SR guideline.[11] These are often specific, fundamental principles that specify some kind of minimal performance level or starting point for an organisation for the respective SR core subjects. According to ISO 26000, under the core subject 'The environment', an organisation has to respect and promote several environmental principles, among which are the precautionary approach and the polluter pays principle.

Did you know...

The US Geological Survey has calculated that 97% of water on Earth is salt water and only 3% is fresh water. Slightly over two-thirds of this fresh water is frozen in glaciers and polar ice caps.[12]

The second and fourth principles of the aforementioned environmental principles are based on the Rio Declaration on Environment and Development,[13] an authoritative international sustainability declaration of the UN, from 1992.[14] Other principles related to CSR core subjects are, for

---

11 A few of these principles will be discussed in more detail in Chapter 6, which deals with SR core subjects and SR issues.

12 ga.water.usgs.gov/edu/waterdistribution.html, accessed 12 April 2011.

13 www.un.org/documents/ga/conf151/aconf15126-1annex1.htm, accessed 12 April 2011.

14 Principle 2: 'States have, in accordance with the Charter of the United Nations and the principles of international law, the sovereign right to exploit their own resources pursuant to their own environmental and developmental policies, and the responsibility to ensure that activities within their jurisdiction or control do not cause damage to the environment of other States or of areas beyond the limits of national jurisdiction.' Principle 4: 'In order to achieve sustainable development, environmental protection shall constitute an integral part of the development process and cannot be considered in isolation from it.'

example, the inalienability, universality and indivisibility of human rights, the principles underlying the Guidelines for Consumer Protection of the UN[15] (such as user safety, redress and respect for the right to privacy) and the Millennium Development Goals[16] (such as reduction of child mortality and the fight against HIV/AIDS, malaria and other diseases—also see Annex 5).

4.4 **Description of the general SR principles**

In this section the general SR principles as specified in ISO 26000 are described. A short explanation on the principles is provided, after which the expectations for organisations according to the respective principles are described.

4.4.1 Accountability

The principle of accountability involves both the taking of responsibility by organisations for their effects on society and the environment, and being accountable for these effects. Hence, the principle of accountability touches the core of CSR: responsibility and accountability are two sides of the same coin (see Chapter 2). This is clear from the list of principles in which the concept of accountability is defined.[17] The explanation and clarification that ISO 26000 gives for the principle itself, also addresses this dual meaning.[18]

The responsibility and accountability of an organisation relate to both those that experience the direct effects of its decisions and activities and on society as a whole because of the effects of the organisation on the communities in which it operates. The degree to which an organisation is responsible and accountable can vary, according to the guideline, but the greater an organisation's influence, the greater it should take care in guaranteeing the quality of its decisions and supervision.

---

15 www.un.org/esa/sustdev/sdissues/consumption/cpp1225.htm, accessed 12 April 2011.

16 www.un.org/millenniumgoals, accessed 12 April 2011.

17 '[. . .] State of being answerable for decisions and activities to the organisation's governing bodies, legal authorities and, more broadly, its other stakeholders' (ISO 2010: 2).

18 The guideline defines the principle as follows (ISO 2010: 10): '[A]n organisation should be accountable for its impacts on society, the economy and the environment.' And adds to this (ISO 2010: 11): 'Accountability also encompasses accepting responsibility where wrongdoing has occurred, taking the appropriate measures to remedy the wrongdoing and taking action to prevent it from being repeated.'

Accountability is also about accepting responsibility for wrongdoing, taking measures to remedy this and undertaking actions in order to prevent this from occurring again. According to this principle, an organisation should take responsibility, and be accountable, for the effects and consequences (both on the environment and on society) of its decisions and activities. For a complete overview of expectations that ISO 26000 specifies towards organisations on the principle of accountability, see page 10 of the ISO 26000 standard.

Did you know...

A 2007 survey by British Telecom found that nearly half of young professionals would choose to avoid working for an employer that showed poor SR. Over one-third of respondents to the survey said that working for a responsible employer was more important to them than the salary they earned.[19]

4.4.2 Transparency

According to this principle an organisation should be transparent about decisions and activities that affect society and the environment. Being transparent means that an organisation has to openly communicate on its policies, decisions and activities (e.g. in sustainability reports and through its website). It doesn't, however, have to publish policies, decisions and activities that could be construed as being competitively sensitive information—this would be unreasonable to expect, of course. It does, however, include, among other things, the known and probable effects of such decisions and activities on society and the environment. Moreover, the information should be quickly and easily available and directly accessible to those that have encountered or could be affected by the activities of the organisation. It is also stressed that the information should be understandable to stakeholders, timely, factual, and be presented in a clear and objective manner (ISO 2010: 11).

According to this principle, an organisation should, among other things, be transparent about the purpose, type and location(s) of its activities, the impacts of its activities and decisions on its stakeholders and society as a whole, its performance on relevant SR issues, and the way in which stakeholders have been identified and engaged. For the full list of expectations that ISO 26000 specifies towards organisations on the principle of transparency, see pages 10 and 11 of the ISO 26000 standard.

---

19 www.mallenbaker.net/csr/page.php?Story_ID=1881, accessed 12 April 2011.

4.4.3 Ethical behaviour

The principle of ethical behaviour encompasses the honesty, equity and integrity of an organisation's actions. An organisation is supposed to behave ethically at all times whenever it concerns people, animals and society as a whole. Furthermore, the organisation is expected to commit itself to addressing the interests of its stakeholders (ISO 2010: 11-12).

According to this principle, an organisation should actively promote ethical behaviour by, among other things, the adoption and application of ethical standards that fit the organisation, the consequent observance of the implementation of these standards by all relevant stakeholders, and the creation of structures and mechanisms to monitor, enforce and report on ethical behaviour. For the full list of expectations that ISO 26000 specifies towards organisations on the principle of ethical behaviour, see pages 11 and 12 of the ISO 26000 standard.

Did you know...

A poll conducted by UK's alternative consumer organisation Ethical Consumer in 2009 showed that politicians and environmental activists consider patio heaters and short-haul flights as being the least ethical products and services from the last 20 years.[20]

4.4.4 Respect for stakeholder interests

This principle deals with respecting, considering and responding to the interests of stakeholders. This is clearly in line with the strong stakeholder orientation of ISO 26000. The topics of stakeholder identification and stakeholder engagement comprise a separate chapter in the guideline (see Chapter 5).

According to this principle, an organisation should, among other things, identify the organisation's stakeholders, recognise and take into account their interests, and respond to concerns that are expressed by stakeholders. For the full list of expectations that ISO 26000 specifies towards organisations on the principle of respect for stakeholder interests, see page 12 of the ISO 26000 standard.

---

20 www.ethicalconsumer.org/AboutUs/20thBirthday/lovethisbanthat.aspx, accessed 12 April 2011.

4.4.5 Respect for the rule of law

This principle states that it is mandatory for an organisation to respect the rule of law. ISO 26000 states that compliance with laws and rules is essential in order to do business in a socially responsible way.[21]

According to this principle, an organisation should, among other things, make sure that it operates according to what is required by law and be informed about all of its legal obligations. For the full list of expectations that ISO 26000 specifies towards organisations on the principle of respect for the rule of law, see pages 12 and 13 of the ISO 26000 standard.

Did you know...

In Maine, after January 14, people will be fined for having Christmas decorations still up.[22]

4.4.6 Respect for international norms of behaviour

In conjunction with complying with the rule of law, an organisation should respect international norms of behaviour. According to this principle, an organisation should, among other things, refrain from activities or relationships that are not in line with international norms of behaviour and operate consistently with these norms in situations or countries in which the law does not provide for minimum safeguards, both environmentally and socially. For the full list of expectations that ISO 26000 specifies towards organisations on the principle of respect for international norms of behaviour, see page 13 of the ISO 26000 standard.

Did you know...

A study conducted by Robert Half Finance & Accounting in 2006 showed that Dutch employees believed themselves to be more productive if they had their own office. It also concluded that employees abroad tend to work harder when they have access to a company fitness programme and had a good computer at their disposal.[23]

4.4.7 Respect for human rights

This principle states that an organisation should respect human rights, and should acknowledge and recognise both the importance and the universality of human rights. According to this principle, an organisation should, among other

---

21 'In the context of social responsibility, respect for the rule of law means that an organisation complies with all applicable laws and regulations. This implies that it should take steps to be aware of applicable laws and regulations, to inform those within the organisation of their obligation to observe and to implement measures' (ISO 2010: 12).

22 www.dumblaws.com/laws/united-states/maine, accessed 12 April 2011.

23 www.personeelsnet.nl/dossier.php?Id=2896&waar=3, accessed 12 April 2011.

things, respect and foster the contents of the International Bill of Human Rights and not take advantage of situations in which human rights are (at risk of being) compromised. For the full list of expectations that ISO 26000 specifies towards organisations on the principle of respect for human rights, see pages 13 and 14 of the ISO 26000 standard.

4.5 **Final words**

The different SR principles that are defined by ISO 26000 and that have been explained in this chapter are not all of the same nature. One principle deals with the way in which SR has to be implemented, while the other focuses on the behaviour of employees during the execution of their tasks. In addition, it can be concluded that, apart from the principles formulated by ISO 26000, other, no less relevant principles, can apply to the SR policy of an organisation as well: respect for future generations; founding SR priorities based on the idea of sustainability impact; and striving for continuous improvement. This idea plus the starting point of ISO 26000 that every organisation should engage in SR in its own, unique way, depending on its organisational characteristics and external environment, offers organisations opportunity and legitimacy to formulate their own SR principles.

Did you know...

According to a report by the WWF, China's biocapacity—the area actually available to produce renewable resources and absorb CO_2 emissions—is among the world's lowest. Although in 2007, the per capita footprint of the average Chinese person was 18% lower than the global level, it was two times greater than its available biocapacity.

Interlude III
Myths and misunderstandings about ISO 26000: Part 2

III.1 **Introduction**

Following on from the previous Interludes, we draw attention here to three additional myths and misunderstandings about ISO 26000. These are:

- ISO 26000 is certifiable

- ISO 26000 is a simple checklist

- ISO 26000 replaces existing CSR-related standards.

III.2 **ISO 26000 is not certifiable (at least, not yet)**

ISO 26000 is not certifiable in its current form and it never will be. There are no institutions or organisations that are able to file an ISO 26000 certificate based on a successful independent audit of an organisation's SR initiative. There is no norm or document available within an ISO 26000 'series' that specifies how an organisation can improve its performance in a way similar to other ISO norms.[1]

Organisations cannot claim that they 'comply with ISO 26000' or that they 'fulfil the requirements of ISO 26000'. Neither can they attempt to demonstrate compliance with an ISO 26000 logo, stamp or other visual sign. Instead, an organisation can state that its SR policy 'is based on ISO 26000' or that its SR policy has been developed and implemented 'according to ISO 26000'. However, the approach ISO 26000 suggests can be integrated in other management systems that are based on certifiable standards such as ISO 9001 or ISO 14001.

Having said this, and despite the often-heard complaint that organisations suffer from a certain certification fatigue, there appears to be a need, especially among enterprises, to develop a certifiable version of ISO 26000. The study by the IISD (Perera 2008) indicated that respondents were interested in knowing how they could demonstrate that they were working in accordance with ISO 26000 and communicate this to other parties. Moreover, they shared the opinion that certain compliance mechanisms (such as certification) would be essential for a worldwide adoption of ISO 26000. The results from the research carried out by Brandsma *et al.* (2009) showed something similar: over 65% of the respondents felt that it would be desirable to develop a certificate or another kind of 'stamp' that would enable organisations to demonstrate that they operate and act in a socially responsible way. One reason for this is that organisations want to increase the credibility of their SR initiatives. A certificate is tangible proof of achievements in a subject that is perceived by many organisations as being soft, intangible or even vague. ISO 26000 appears to recognise this concern and points to other options already available.

The fact that ISO 26000 is not certifiable now does not mean that it will never be certifiable. Another type of standard, based on ISO 26000, should, in our opinion, be developed for the purpose of certification. In fact, the possibility of developing a certifiable version of ISO 26000 is currently the subject of discussions within different ISO forums. It is expected that large consultancies and certifying institutions will take the initiative to develop a SR certificate based on ISO 26000 (and let their reputations add value to the certificate). In for instance Denmark, Portugal and the Netherlands this is already the case and from this fact alone it can be concluded that there appears to be a

---

1 This is clarified in one of the first points made by ISO 26000 (ISO 2010: 1): 'It is not intended or appropriate for certification purposes or regulatory or contractual use. Any offer to certify, or claims to be certified, to ISO 26000 would be a misrepresentation of the intent and purpose and a misuse of this International Standard.'

demand for such a certificate. In line with a desire to increase the credibility of their own SR efforts, larger enterprises are increasingly inquiring into their suppliers' SR efforts and there is a need for an instrument or a mechanism to be able to evaluate those efforts in a proper way. Governments may also want to use such a mechanism as part of their objectives in the field of sustainable procurement.[2] Moreover, it is expected that other certifiable schemes and standards, such as SA8000 and several eco-labels, will make certain aspects of ISO 26000 required elements of their certificates.

Finally, the fact that ISO 26000 is not certifiable does not mean that ISO 26000 is not eligible for auditing. One can expect that large and specialised consultancies will offer audit services. In addition, different forms of auditing are possible such as peer-to-peer auditing. This means that an enterprise that has based its SR policy on ISO 26000 could be audited by one or more companies with experience in that field. Combinations of these two forms are also possible (see also Chapter 9).

III.3 **ISO 26000 is a checklist**

ISO 26000 does not offer a simple checklist and it is not possible to check off tasks or items. One of the disadvantages of certifiable standards is that they encourage compliance behaviour and risk legitimising a box-ticking approach and culture that aims only for the minimum requirements. This contrasts with the ambition that ISO 26000 clearly intends to instil in its users.

ISO 26000 corresponds much better with our proposition for SR 2.0—a new generation of SR which dispenses with checklists to define social responsibilities, but gives organisations the space to interpret SR in their own way. ISO 26000 provides and defines SR principles to guide users towards an organisation-specific SR policy. Apart from engaging with stakeholders and taking account of the necessary requirements for recognising the core subjects in ISO 26000, organisations have a relatively free rein in organising their policies on social responsibility to create a unique SR profile.[3]

---

2 It is noted here that a requirement, for instance as formulated by a client, such as 'operating according to ISO 26000' as part of criteria for sustainable procurement is not in line with the intention of ISO 26000, as the guideline is not intended for contractual use.

3 The guideline states that (ISO 2010: 8): '[w]hen reviewing all seven core subjects and identifying the relevant issues, the organisation's own context, conditions,

III.4 **ISO 26000 replaces all existing CSR-related norms, standards and guidelines**

ISO 26000 is not a substitute for any other norm, guideline, code, convention or standard of any kind.[4]

Of course, ISO 26000 does not replace any laws. The guideline does recognise and refer to certain parts of a number of different standards—often by means of texts that can be characterised as 'in the spirit of', but sometimes also by literally quoting texts from the applicable standards. ISO 26000 can hence be seen as a guideline that describes the common ground of several standards that are focused on individual core subjects and issues that are brought together under the umbrella of ISO 26000. ISO 26000 is consistent with many international conventions, norms and guidelines, such as ISO 9001 and ISO 14001, the GRI guidelines for sustainability reporting and the AA1000 series for creating stakeholder engagement.

The most important function of ISO 26000 in this sense is as a framework—all kinds of standards, and the demands and requirements specified within those standards, can be found within the guideline. In addition, ISO 26000 gives organisations the opportunity to connect their SR initiatives to CSR-related structures, systems and procedures that already exist within their organisations. This is a logical starting point, as CSR is not something completely new for most (large) organisations. The challenge that ISO 26000 asks organisations to face is to make the linkages, join up the dots and create a structured, consistent SR initiative.

---

resources and stakeholder interests should be taken into account, recognising that all core subjects but not all issues will be relevant for every organisations.'

4 The guideline explicitly states at the beginning of the document (ISO 2010: 1): 'It is intended to [. . .] complement other instruments and initiatives for social responsibility, not to replace them.'

5

Stakeholder identification and engagement

5.1 **Introduction**

One of the general CSR principles within ISO 26000 concerns respecting stakeholder interests. Identifying stakeholders, knowing their expectations and enabling stakeholder engagement therefore play an important role in the guideline as they are a key to understanding, addressing and implementing social responsibility.[1]

Stakeholders are seen as a starting point for CSR policies and fulfil an essential role in determining an organisation's social responsibilities. Therefore, ISO 26000 is full of references to stakeholders and stakeholder involvement, dedicating an entire clause to this concept, Clause 5. The guideline is very clear: ISO 26000 stresses the importance of a stakeholder orientation in an organisation's approach towards SR.

This chapter starts by examining the relationships between organisations, its stakeholders and society in the broadest sense of the word—relationships every organisation should understand. It explains how ISO 26000 defines stakeholders and how stakeholder interests can be in line with, but also in contrast with, the interests of society. Subsequently, the concept of

---

1 'Stakeholder identification and engagement are central to addressing an organisation's social responsibility' (ISO 2010: 16).

stakeholder identification is explained and continues by illustrating how stakeholder interests can be identified. Additionally, this chapter offers a number of instruments to map the most important stakeholders of an organisation. The second part of the chapter focuses on the creation of stakeholder engagement. This topic receives attention because it is perceived as essential by ISO 26000 in order to develop an effective SR policy and because it frequently reoccurs as a material issue in the different SR core subjects in the guideline.

5.2 Relationships between the organisation, stakeholders and society

The previous chapter has shown that respecting stakeholder interests is one of the general SR principles specified in ISO 26000. This is seen as a fundamental part of SR—respecting stakeholder interests is a starting point for any SR policy. However, there are other important interests as well. To identify its social responsibility properly, an organisation should, according to ISO 26000, understand three specific relationships. First is the relationship between the organisation and society. The effects of an organisation's activities, products and services on society should be central, as should the expectations that society has regarding responsible and sustainable behaviour by the organisation in the light of these effects. The actions and expectations that ISO 26000 specifies for core subjects and issues can assist an organisation in this (see Chapter 6). Second, an organisation should understand the relationship it has with its stakeholders. In order to do so, it first needs to be aware of who its stakeholders actually are and, second, be aware of their expectations, interests, demands and wishes. The fact that there are individuals, groups and organisations that (can be) influence(d by) the decisions and activities of an organisation, means that they have an interest.[2]

However, sometimes stakeholders are not aware of the fact that they *are* stakeholders of an organisation. This can also be the case the other way around—an organisation does not have a clear idea of who its stakeholders are. Stakeholders' expectations, as emphasised by ISO 26000, are not necessarily the same as expectations of society. Here is the third relationship that

---

2 'Stakeholders are organisations or individuals that have one or more interests in any decision or activity of an organisation. Because these interests can be affected by an organisation, a relationship with the organisation is created' (ISO 2010: 17).

needs to be understood: the relationship with society as a whole. For example, there can be cases in which the interests of stakeholders are opposed to the interests of society or in which stakeholders claim to represent a certain kind of social interest (for example, witnessing the size of their constituents), but it does not appear to be the case to the degree they claim. For instance, many environmental and animal rights activists claim they represent nature and animals (or society's interest in these matters), but how do we know they actually do? In other cases, stakeholder interests do represent social interests. ISO 26000 mentions the example of a supplier that wants to have its invoices paid. This is a specific stakeholder interest, but the (timely) compliance with such contractual obligations is certainly of importance to society as a whole (see Box 5.1). An organisation should understand the relationship between interests of stakeholders that are affected by the organisation on the one hand, and the importance of society's interests on the other.[3]

Moreover, there is also a problem of representation: the person or thing that influences or can be influenced by an organisation is not always able to represent itself. Obvious examples are children, animals, the environment and future generations. Stakeholder interests are in that case always a 'derived' interest. Therefore, it is always useful for an organisation to consider whose or which interest a certain stakeholder represents.

5.2.1 Interaction and influence

When determining its social responsibilities, an organisation should take into account all of these three relationships and balance the interests, expectations, demands and wishes that play a part. Recognising the stakeholders of an organisation is inherent in recognising the social responsibilities of an organisation. Therefore, organisations should take this into account when different SR core subjects are addressed (see Chapter 6). Taking into account stakeholder interests and the interactions with other organisations helps an organisation do this and can serve as a basis for formulating its SR priorities.[4]

---

3 'Although stakeholders are part of society, they may have an interest that is not consistent with the expectations of society. Stakeholders have particular interests with regard to the organisation that can be distinguished from societal expectations of socially responsible behaviour regarding any issue' (ISO 2010: 14).

4 'When recognising the core subjects and issues of its social responsibility, an organisation is helped by considering interactions with other organisations. An organisation should consider the impact of its decisions and activities on stakeholders' (ISO 2010: 16).

Box 5.1 **Bad payers: socially irresponsible?**

Source: www.volkskrant.nl and www.rtlnieuws.nl

The Dutch government abides very poorly by agreements on paying. One in every five payments by municipalities, cities, provinces and the national government do not take place within the agreed timeframe, as research conducted by Dun & Bradstreet shows. The Dutch government occupies first position in the ranking list of 'bad payers', followed closely by Belgium, France, the UK, Germany and Italy. At the end of 2008 Dutch Prime Minister Balkenende committed to substantially shorten payment periods in order to alleviate the consequences of the economic crisis for businesses.

Interestingly, from the analysis performed by Dun & Bradstreet, it has become clear that the Netherlands occupies this dubious position from its strict payment ethics, as the Dutch government promises to pay its bills over a relatively short term. Of all countries included in the research, payment ethics is the strongest in the Netherlands: it is often the case that debtor and creditor agree to pay bills within a period of 25 to 40 days, while in Italy this term is typically 60 to 100 days. After 90 days only 0.8% of the bills that have been sent to the Dutch government have not been paid, while in Italy, for instance, the percentage is 4%.

Dutch companies themselves do not take payment obligations too seriously either, it appears: over 75% of companies do not pay within the agreed timeframe. On average, Dutch companies pay within 17.7 days after the agreed deadline. This is 1% above the European average.

ISO 26000 finds it important in these stakeholder relationships that an organisation uses its influence to encourage stakeholders to address SR. If necessary, an organisation should even terminate relationships with stakeholders such as suppliers or business partners. The concept of the 'sphere of influence' is such an important topic within ISO 26000 that the guideline devotes a number of paragraphs to it.[5]

---

5   This topic will also be dealt with in more detail in Chapter 7.

5.3 **Identifying stakeholders and their interests**

The meaning of the term 'stakeholder' is extremely broad. Organisations can have many stakeholders, varying from individuals to society as a whole and encompassing abstractions such as 'the environment'. In general, stakeholders are divided into internal and external groups as well as into primary (market-related) and secondary (non-market-related) categories. The goal of such categorisation is to offer organisations structure and provide them with an overview of the possible interests of, and relationships with and between, stakeholders. Examples of typical stakeholders are employees, clients, shareholders, consumers, suppliers, partners, competitors, trade unions, citizens, NGOs, scientific and educational institutions, governments and the media. Often by categorising stakeholders into these dimensions a first prioritisation of stakeholder relations takes place.

ISO 26000 emphasises that the relationship between an organisation and its stakeholders exists, irrespective of the fact that these parties are aware or unaware of it. Moreover, the guideline states that not all stakeholders of an organisation belong to organised groups that aim to represent and promote certain interests. Many stakeholders are not organised and can be easily ignored or neglected by an organisation. This is especially true of vulnerable groups, such as children, women and disabled people. Figure 5.1 shows an example of the stakeholders of a local government.

According to ISO 26000, determining an organisation's sustainability impact is the most important way to identify stakeholders. Insight into the effects that can be caused by the activities, products and services of an organisation, and insight into its ecological and social footprint, together provide the largest part of the answer to the question of who an organisation's stakeholders are. This also clearly means that the relevant stakeholders are not the same for every organisation.

In conjunction with the method that an organisation uses to measure its sustainability impact (e.g. carbon footprint analysis), ISO 26000 states that an organisation can ask itself several questions in order to map its stakeholders. For instance, when an organisation looks at its legal obligations, it quickly becomes clear who some of its most important stakeholders are. Also, an organisation can look at the people, organisations or other actors that are affected or impacted by its decisions and activities. In addition, it may be helpful for an organisation to make an analysis of its value chain and dependency relationships in order to derive other key relevant stakeholders.

Figure 5.1 **Illustration of stakeholders of a local government**

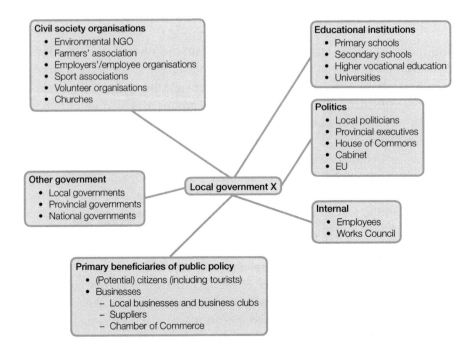

In addition to this, an organisation can ask itself the following questions:

- Who cares about our activities?

- Who has ever filed a complaint about us?

- Who is able to help us look differently at a problem we have or at the consequences of our activities?

- Who monitors, judges or reports on us?

5.3.1 Stakeholder interests

As concluded earlier on, every stakeholder brings a unique interest. Despite the fact that the concepts 'stakeholders' and 'society' do not necessarily mean the same thing, they have a clear relationship.[6]

6 For example, ISO 26000 notes that (ISO 2010: 17): 'The interest of most stakeholders can be related to the social responsibility of the organisation and often are very similar to some of the interests of society. An example is the interest of a property owner whose property loses value because of a new source of pollution.'

Interests can differ enormously and sometimes even conflict—even within the same stakeholder group. 'The challenge of stakeholder management lies in reaching responsible decisions through stakeholder dialogue, knowing that as an organisation, you cannot always please everybody', according to Goodijk (2006). In other cases, these interests are the same. This is, for example, the case for employees and shareholders—both have an interest in an organisation being successful while also having different, additional interests. A stakeholder probably has or represents several interests. In this case as well, these interests can be opposed to each other. ISO 26000 gives the example of inhabitants of a community that experience both the positive effects of the presence of a company (such as employment) and the negative effects of that same company (such as pollution). Stakeholder interests, according to ISO 26000, are certainly not restricted to financial and legal issues. Sometimes it can be about the right or the opportunity to be heard by the organisation.

In order to map stakeholder interests, an organisation can ask itself in which ways stakeholders experience the effects of its activities. From a SR point of view, the best way to find out the relevance of an interest is by determining the relationship between the interest and sustainable development, according to ISO 26000. Here, the guideline offers a good starting point, since many interests and expectations of stakeholders are included in the SR core subjects and issues, as for instance specified in the actions and expectation the guideline formulates for each of the issues. However, there is not an exhaustive overview and the examples given are, at least partly, expectations of society in a broad sense rather than of specific stakeholders. Therefore, an organisation will have to make additional efforts to get a complete view of the expectations, interests, demands and wishes of stakeholders, for instance by extensively surveying its stakeholders or conducting stakeholder panels. Additional questions that an organisation could ask itself are, for example:

Did you know . . .

Research conducted by the Boston College Centre for Corporate Citizenship shows that 54% of US business leaders report that attention to corporate citizenship efforts is even more important in a recession. Only one-third of executives who responded to the survey say greater regulatory oversight by the federal government is an important part of solving the current economic crisis and creating a more stable economy.

- What are the minimal expectations of our most important stakeholders?

- What are the wishes of our most important stakeholders?

- What advantages can a stakeholder experience from our activities, products or services?

- What disadvantages can a stakeholder experience from our activities, products or services?

- What possible reasons are there for conflict with a stakeholder?

- What do our stakeholders expect of our SR performance?

Of course, an organisation can also ask these questions of the respective stakeholders. In that way it directly starts to create stakeholder engagement (see §5.4). Figure 5.2 indicates the stakeholder interests of a UK-based transportation company.

Figure 5.2 **Stakeholders of a transportation company and their interests**
Source: Volvo Group Sustainability Report 2009

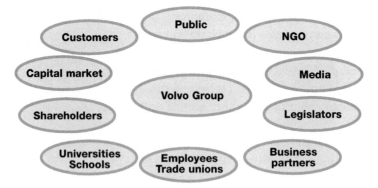

Organisations should always consider the legitimacy of their stakeholders' interests, demands, expectations and wishes. Which are reasonable, desirable, suitable and/or justified? In general stakeholder demands tend to be perceived as legitimate when they are supported by a large group, are more supported (or ratified) socially and/or are better argued by the stakeholder(s). Shareholders, for instance, can point to the financial risks they experience, activist groups are likely to be concerned with social or environmental problems, consumers interests may focus on the quality or safety of products, and employees may be preoccupied with the importance of job security. Some of the interests, demands, expectations and wishes of stakeholders are reflected in the SR core subjects and issues as described in ISO 26000. Because these are based on international conventions, guidelines and standards, they have a certain legitimacy.

5.3.1.1 An ISO norm for stakeholder analysis?

The importance of making a good stakeholder analysis is not limited to the field of SR. That is why, in 2009, ISO crafted a proposal to develop a norm for performing stakeholder analyses.

The goal of this norm would be to offer practical methods and tools for the identification and involvement of stakeholders, with the goal of developing a substantiated basis for supported decisions. The norm contains principles for planning, designing, communicating and executing a timely stakeholder analysis and approach. The points of attention for the decision to perform a consultation can become part of the norm as well. The norm can be a useful addition to several standards. For example, the ISO proposal refers to ISO 26000, ISO 9001, ISO 14001 and ISO 10001 (customer satisfaction). For any of these standards a good stakeholder analysis is an important ingredient.

This norm could offer a practical tool for performing a stakeholder analysis. It can also be broadly applied, ranging from 'simple' information supplied in a consultation to 'complex' broad processes and projects with a multi-stakeholder focus. Aimed at both the public and private sector, the norm is not meant as guidance for corporate governance and representative democracy.

5.3.2 Stakeholder importance and degree of influence

It would, of course, be fanciful to claim that every stakeholder is equally important to an organisation. To determine the importance of a stakeholder, the concept of impact can serve an organisation well. In line with ISO 26000 one could use the rule that the greater the effects of an organisation's activities are for a stakeholder, the more important that stakeholder is. Of course, this applies even more when it relates to sustainability effects. The effects on a stakeholder can be determined as being large when a clear relationship with sustainable development exists (stakeholders that represent a specific sustainability theme or aspect, such as child workers or endangered species). Because of the emphasis ISO 26000 puts on so-called vulnerable groups, it can also be stated that these groups should be included in the group of priority stakeholders. Examples of such stakeholder groups are female, handicapped and migrant workers.

However, there are also other criteria to define, in order to determine the importance of a stakeholder or its interest(s). One obvious example is the 'sphere of influence' of a stakeholder.

This influence is, among others, determined by the political, social and/or economic position of a stakeholder, but also the degree to which a stakeholder

is organised, plays a role or has informal power
(e.g. trade unions or environmental NGOs). If the
organisation is dependent upon a stakeholder
group in reaching its goals, then the stakeholder
has a good deal of power. One well-known way
for assessing the power of stakeholder groups is
the matrix developed by management scholars
Johnson and Scholes (1999) which typifies stake-
holders by means of their influence and their importance. Still, ISO 26000
states that all types of stakeholder should receive an organisation's attention
to a certain degree (see Fig. 5.3). An organisation can use this matrix to plot
different stakeholders and, consequently, determine the kind of relationship
it has with them.

Figure 5.3 **Stakeholder matrix**

Source: Johnson and Scholes 1999

Importance	High	Keep informed	Important stakeholders
	Low	Minimal effort	Keep satisfied
		Low	High

Influence on the organisation

If the willingness of a stakeholder to cooperate with an organisation on SR
issues is low, and it mainly aims for confrontation, its importance as a stakeholder only increases. Such factors should also be taken into account when
determining the relationship that an organisation enters into with its different stakeholders (see also §5.4).

The overview (Table 5.1) as well as the matrix (Fig. 5.4) provide simple tools to
help organisations get an idea of their stakeholders and evaluate their interests.

Table 5.1 **Instrument to get an idea of stakeholders and their interests**

Stake-holder	Impor-tance	Effect of the organisation on stakeholder	Degree to which the stakeholder is important for the organisation's success	Degree of influence on the organisation
X	Y	❑ unknown ❑ negative ❑ neutral ❑ positive	❑ unknown ❑ hardly ❑ average ❑ large ❑ essential	❑ unknown ❑ hardly ❑ average ❑ large ❑ decisive

Figure 5.4 **Instrument to typify stakeholders based on two
characteristics**

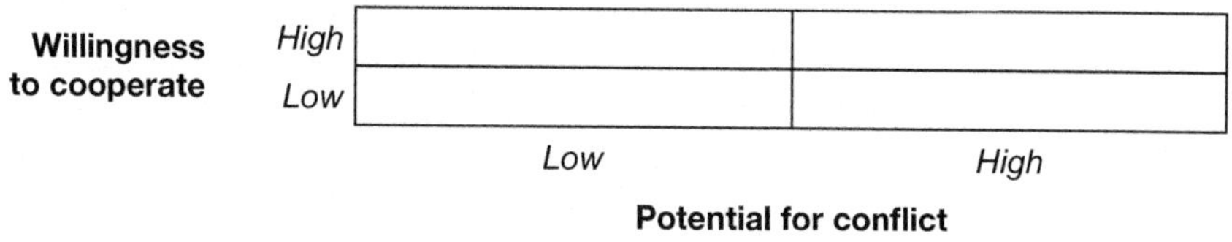

Willingness to cooperate	*High*		
	Low		
		Low	*High*
		Potential for conflict	

5.4 **Creating stakeholder engagement**

In earlier draft versions of ISO 26000 stakeholder engagement was integrally woven through the text and into several SR core subjects and issues, which underlined the importance of the topic. Despite the fact that the importance of stakeholder engagement has not decreased and ISO 26000, as a whole, has certainly not become less stakeholder-oriented, the decision was made to emphasise the role of stakeholder engagement in the guideline by giving it its own section.

The reasoning behind this is that stakeholder engagement helps an organisation address its social responsibilities by creating the conditions for informed decision-making and can produce advantages in a variety of ways. ISO 26000 specifies numerous reasons to engage with stakeholders. These include reaching informed decisions (by taking into account the effects of its activities in its decision-making), including stakeholders in the process of performance evaluation, reconciling or preventing conflicts, aligning interests and expectations, integrating different perspectives and developing partnerships (ISO 2010: 18). Other reasons include: minimising the possibility of reputational damage or bad press (from a risk management perspective); the possibility of generating new ideas for products or services; building a critical sounding board; and increasing the credibility of an organisation's SR initiatives.

As has become clear from the previous section, the creation of a process of stakeholder engagement can be an excellent way to map stakeholders' expectations as well as those of society as a whole. However, according to ISO 26000, that is not always necessary since some stakeholder expectations have been institutionalised within the law, culture or societal norms.[7] In fact, ISO 26000

---

7 'In most situations an organisation will already know, or can easily learn, society's expectations of the way the organisation should address its impacts. In such

as a guideline that is largely based on many international conventions, guidelines and standards, is an example of this in itself.

ISO 26000 states that an organisation should provide for the development of a fair and decent process of stakeholder engagement, based on engaging the most relevant and representative stakeholders for the issue under discussion. Here, the guideline again acknowledges the idea of an organisation-specific SR profile—an organisation should identify and focus its main SR efforts on the stakeholders that are most relevant to it.

The guideline also states that an organisation should not give preference or favour to any particular organised group to garner a more friendly stance towards its own goals (ISO 2010: 19). An organisation should also not, by supporting such groups, cultivate the impression of having a dialogue partner, when this partner is in fact not independent. An organisation should also be aware of the interests and needs of its stakeholders and facilitate open dialogue. Finally, ISO 26000 adds that the active engagement of stakeholders is based on trust and goes beyond public relations. Stakeholder engagement is only effective according to the guideline when the organisation and its stakeholders have a mutual belief that they are engaging in dialogue for the right reasons. This means that the essence of the dialogue should concern aspects that are strongly related to sustainable development, are of sufficient importance for the parties involved and that the interests of all parties are clearly formulated from the start.

5.4.1 Methods and tools to engage stakeholders

So how, exactly, does an organisation engage successfully with its stakeholders? What should an organisation do? According to ISO 26000, stakeholder engagement comprises a dialogue between the organisation and one or more of its stakeholders. The origin of the dialogue is not necessarily important and can be for many reasons—because of a new development, a change in activities or by special invitation from the organisation itself. The fact that there *is* a dialogue at least implies interaction. Interaction is therefore the basis of stakeholder engagement in the view of ISO 26000; and it suggests a number of methods and tools—both formal and informal—both for individual stakeholders and collective negotiations, such as stakeholder panels, seminars,

---

circumstances, it need not rely on engagement with specific stakeholders to understand these expectations, although the stakeholder engagement process can provide other benefits. Society's expectations are also found in laws or regulations, widely accepted social or cultural expectations, and established best practices with regarding specific matters' (ISO 2010: 18).

conferences and workshops, roundtables, advisory committees or internet forums.

Many organisations have already been working on stakeholder engagement. Interactive policy development, which has by now become common for many governments, is an example of this. Box 5.2 offers an illustration of the ways an international beverages company works on stakeholder engagement.

Engagement can be both general and specific. Unilaterally supplying information, for example, in the form of periodically informing or updating stakeholders by means of public media such as press releases and newsletters can be part of the range of instruments that an organisation can deploy to create stakeholder engagement. Such forms of information supply do not necessarily comply with the criterion that ISO 26000 formulates for stakeholder engagement, but can still be useful. At the other end of the spectrum a stakeholder group might be offered a key role in the governance structure of an organisation. Supervisory functions and employee councils are examples of this. Another example of a recent practice is engaging stakeholders in the process of verifying company sustainability reports.

Other frequently used instruments are stakeholder panels and stakeholder consultations. An increasing number of organisations are creating stakeholder panels which include priority stakeholder groups to deal with pressing SR topics. Currently, there is a trend among companies (such as Camelot, BP, Shell, Burger King, Coca-Cola, GE, BHP Billiton, Lafarge, Dow Chemical, Reuters, Unilever and Nestlé) to include formal stakeholder panels in their governance structure. However, size is not the issue here. Any organisation, of any size and operating in any sector, could find that a stakeholder panel is a useful instrument. It is not essential that all stakeholders have to be represented, and there are less formal ways in which they can be organised and directed towards a limited number of topics. Box 5.3 shows a step-by-step guide for the development of an effective stakeholder panel.

What applies to stakeholder panels also applies to undertaking a stakeholder consultation: any organisation can approach its stakeholders and ask whether they want to engage in a dialogue about expectations regarding the social responsibilities of the organisation. When an organisation decides to perform a stakeholder consultation, it should consider how the consultation will function (for example, by means of face-to-face conversations, focus groups or via an online application), how the results will be used and what the consultees can expect in return. Box 5.4 lists some questions that an organisation may wish to ask in a stakeholder consultation.

It can also be interesting for an organisation to ask its own management and employees how they think stakeholders will answer these questions.

Box 5.2 Ways in which Fujifilm works on stakeholder engagement

Source: adapted from www.fujifilmholdings.com/en/sustainability/communication/relationship/index.html

Employees

Employees play a central role in the promotion of Fujifilm's CSR activities.

Methods for sustaining dialogue

- Consulting Centres of the Personnel Department and personnel interviews
- Compliance and Sexual Harassment Helpline
- Labour union and regular company meetings
- Stakeholder Dialogue
- Awareness surveys related to making work more satisfying

Suppliers

Our suppliers are important partners who assist us in continuing to offer products that reflect proper regard for safety and the natural environment.

Methods for sustaining dialogue

- Procurement Division (for responding to inquiries)
- FUJIFILM Business Expert (for responding to inquiries)
- Ecology and Quality Management Division (for responding to inquiries)
- Information meetings for suppliers (green procurement, management of chemical content)
- Periodic discussion meetings with our suppliers
- Operation of a materials procurement website

Community (regional societies)

We believe that symbiosis with the community and the preservation of the natural environment are key elements of our CSR as a corporation, especially at those places of business for production operation. We, therefore, promote communication with the community.

Methods for sustaining dialogue

- Consulting centres at each of our factories and offices (for responding to inquiries)
- Meeting related to environmental policy
- Factory visits
- Volunteer activities in the local community
- Lectures and information meetings for community members
- Periodic discussions with local governments (municipal governments and mayors, leaders of local government organisations, and others)

Box 5.3 **Developing a stakeholder panel in five steps**

Source: Chhabara 2009

Step 1: Make a plan

- Be clear about the goal and the focus of the panel
- Connect the panel to other processes in the organisation
- Make sure that there is internal support for the stakeholder panel

Step 2: Set the rules

- Establish the mandate of the panel and formulate the rules of the game

Step 3: Recruit stakeholders

- Panel members should be able to represent the interests and expectations of important stakeholders

Step 4: Support the panel

- Help panel members to get a better understanding of the company's strategy
- Work on building trust
- Stick to promises made about undertaking action

Step 5: Measure success

- Periodically review the panel's progress

Box 5.4 **Questions to ask in a stakeholder consultation**

Introduction

- Generally, what do you expect in the field of SR from the sort of organisation that we are?
- What kind of associations do you have when it comes to SR for our organisation?
- Can you paint a picture of our organisation if we were doing business in a fully socially responsible way?

Contents

- What are the five most important SR focus areas for our organisation according to you?
- What are typical responsibilities of our organisation in the field of 'people' according to you?
- What are typical responsibilities of our organisation in the field of 'planet' according to you?
- What are typical responsibilities of our organisation in the field of 'profit' according to you?

Achievements

- Do you think that our organisation currently does business in a socially responsible way?
- How would you classify our organisation in the field of SR—a champion? a laggard? in-between? Do you also think that this is the most appropriate role for our organisation? If not, what role would fit best?
- Does the SR performance of our organisation meet your expectations and demands? If not, where does our organisation fail in your opinion?
- What are the most important KPIs (key performance indicators) for our organisation in the field of SR according to you?

Ambition

- Does our organisation's SR ambitions meet your expectations? If not, on which topics do these ambitions fall short?
- Where are the largest gaps between the SR ambitions of our organisation and the current situation located according to you?

Influence and cooperation

- What effects do you expect the realisation of the SR ambitions of our organisation to have on your organisation?
- What is your interest in a 'sustainable [your organisation's name]'?
- To what extent is a 'sustainable [your organisation's name]' important for your organisation?
- How can your organisation contribute to the realisation of the SR ambitions of our organisation and vice versa?

Their response can then be compared with that of the stakeholders. This can help clarify the extent to which the organisation has a clear idea of how it is viewed by its stakeholders.

5.5 **Final comment**

ISO 26000 puts great emphasis on stakeholders and their interests, and not without reason. The stakeholders of an organisation experience the (positive and negative) effects of its activities, products and services, have expectations towards it and have demands. These are essential ingredients for developing the SR policy of any organisation. An organisation is constantly interacting with its stakeholders and it should manage these relationships and its social responsibilities well. Therefore, creating stakeholder engagement is important: it fits within the concept of SR as used in ISO 26000 (and in other generally accepted conceptions of (C)SR and offers organisations numerous advantages. Effective stakeholder engagement is thus important for an organisation, and if an organisation wants to obtain maximum value from it, it should properly organise this process, as stated in ISO 26000.[8]

Moreover, it is also important to realise that stakeholder engagement is not a one-off event, but a continuous process, Stakeholders, their interests and expectations, their influence and the ways to actively engage them can and will change over time. Therefore, every organisation should periodically review its policies and activities in the field of stakeholder engagement.

---

8 'Stakeholder engagement is more likely to be meaningful when the following elements are present: a clear purpose for the engagement is understood; the stakeholder's interests have been identified; the relationship that these interests establish between the organisation and the stakeholder is direct or important; the interests of stakeholders are relevant and significant to sustainable development; and the stakeholders have the necessary information and understanding to make their decisions' (ISO 2010: 19).

Interlude IV

Frequently asked questions about ISO 26000

IV.1 **Introduction**

There are many questions about ISO 26000. This interlude brings together some of the most frequently asked and provides answers.[1]

IV.2 **FAQs about ISO 26000**

Question: *Who has developed the guideline?*

Answer: ISO 26000 was written by experts from both developed and developing countries and from a wide range of stakeholder groups represented in the worldwide consultation process (businesses and business associations, governments, trade unions, NGOs, consumers and others) in order for ISO 26000 to represent a balanced overview and contents. These 450 participating experts were part of a dedicated working group called the ISO Working Group on

---

1 These questions and answers are based on examples of FAQs from several sources and organisations, such as the ISO website on ISO 26000 (www.iso.org/sr), websites and documents from different national normalisation institutes, and authorities in the field of quality management as well as the authors' own experiences.

Social Responsibility. This working group, which started in the end of 2004 and is now disbanded as the guideline is finished, was led by the Brazilian and Swedish normalisation institutes.

Question: *Why does ISO use the abbreviation SR ('social responsibility') instead of the more commonly used CSR ('corporate social responsibility')?*

Answer: Although the concept of CSR applies to all types of organisations (not only corporations), taking the 'corporate' out of CSR and labelling it as SR better suited the multi-stakeholder brief and political purposes of ISO 26000. We feel that it is a somewhat artificial way to broaden the CSR concept in order for it to encompass all governmental institutions and other kinds of organisations (such as social organisations) that have an interest in showing their way of working on social responsibility. CSR remains the most often used term in this area.

Question: *A standard for SR in the form of a guideline sounds good, but wouldn't it be wiser to let individual organisations decide for themselves what to do?*

Answer: These days, many companies already have their own programmes, policies and guidelines for SR and these can differ greatly from each other (which, we believe, is essentially a good thing). However, common basic definitions, working methods and ways of evaluating performance could make life easier. This does not necessarily mean reinventing the wheel for organisations already advanced in this area. Rather, it means that all of the spokes of the wheel are identified for all users. ISO 26000 advocates an organisation-specific way of dealing with SR, so in fact organisations can still determine themselves how they deal with SR.

Question: *ISO 26000 is not a norm, but a standard—a guideline, actually. What exactly is a standard?*

Answer: A standard is a document, developed by consensus and approved by an acknowledged institution, which, for the purpose of general and repeated use, provides rules, guidelines or characteristics for activities or results, aimed at achieving an optimal degree of order and structure in a certain context.

Question: *Why would our organisation apply ISO 26000?*

Answer: By far the most important reason for organisations to work with ISO 26000 is because of the help it provides in structuring SR activities: from setting priorities to implementing programmes. It can also enhance the credibility of SR communications.

Question: *How can an organisation refer to the use of ISO 26000?*

Answer: ISO 26000 is a voluntary international standard that offers guidelines for determining social responsibilities and implementing programmes to manage these. Organisations are encouraged by ISO to communicate their use of ISO 26000 in one of the ways described below:

- Our organisation acknowledges ISO 26000 as a reference document which offers guidelines in the field of SR

- Our organisation has used ISO 26000 as a guide to implement SR into our values and ways of working

- To develop its SR policy our organisation has checked the ISO 26000 recommendations for their usefulness

- Our organisation addresses its social responsibility in accordance with ISO 26000

What is impossible to state is that an organisation is ISO 26000-certified.

Question: *Does ISO 26000 include environmental requirements such as those in ISO 14001? Or is ISO 26000 complementary to ISO 14001?*

Answer: ISO 26000 describes several environmental issues that should be taken into account by organisations as part of their SR initiative, such as preventing pollution and preserving natural sources. However, the guideline does not provide an environmental management system, but rather uses ISO 14001 as a reference document which, in turn, can be used by organisations that want to work according to ISO 26000. The use of ISO 14001 is not mandatory, however, for organisations that want to work in accordance with ISO 26000. These standards are indeed complementary.

Question: *Has there been any criticism of ISO 26000?*

Answer: Of course—a good deal of criticism, actually. Criticism is, among other things, directed towards the following points:

- The guideline insufficiently addresses its most important 'market'—SMEs—because the seven core subjects that must be taken into account are not sufficiently relevant to SMEs

- The document is too large to be user-friendly. Few organisations will be engaged by a guideline that has its contents spread over more than 90 pages.

- It is disputed by different types of organisations, such as SMEs, NGOs and industry organisations, that not all seven core subjects are relevant to their organisation. ISO 26000 can be easily abused—or at least used in ways that it is not intended. Governments could make it a requirement for sustainable procurement (which is already the case), certifying institutions could develop an SR certificate that is based directly or indirectly on ISO 26000 (which is also already the case) and enterprises could make it a contractual requirement (which, indeed, practice has also already shown to be true).

Question: *What difficulties do organisations expect in using ISO 26000?*

Answer: Research by Brandsma *et al.* (2009) indicates that organisations expect to have difficulties with the comprehensiveness of the guideline. There are too many expectations and required actions with the core subjects and related issues which will make it hard to apply in practice. In addition, the guideline is perceived as having included too many options and too few concrete requirements. Finally, organisations fear that customers will not recognise the added value of ISO 26000.

Question: *Normalisation institutes in several countries have a committee for CSR. What do these committees do?*

Answer: These committees determined and advised about the input of the respective countries in the development process of ISO 26000 and continue to do so regarding the strategies of international normalisation in the field of SR.

Question: *Are organisations already working with ISO 26000?*

Answer: Yes. There are several organisations, mainly companies, that have experimented with ISO 26000 and are currently working according to the guideline, such as the Brazilian Petrobras or the Australian Dental Association Victorian Branch.

Question: *Isn't it a lot of effort to work according to ISO 26000?*

Answer: Yes and no. ISO 26000 is meant as guidance and in that sense gives advice about how organisations can link it with existing CSR-related structures, systems and procedures. CSR is not a new issue for most large organisations. At the same time, most organisations will have to deal with unfamiliar subjects or fields of attention and will have to accurately define where their sustainability impact lies. This mapping process will probably require the most effort and investment.

Question: *How can I create an overview of the degree to which my organisation already works according to ISO 26000?*

Answer: There are ISO 26000 quick scans available that can offer a first insight into the degree to which an organisation already works in accordance with ISO 26000. Many of these are not yet based on the final version of the SR guideline, but in general they give a good (first) overview. A quick scan of ISO 26000 is available at: www. ISO26000quickscan.nl (Dutch). A slightly adjusted version of this tool is available in Annex 1 of this book.

6

SR core subjects and issues

6.1 **Introduction**

In this chapter the focus is on the SR core subjects and the specified SR issues in ISO 26000. While the SR principles, discussed in Chapter 4 and issues regarding stakeholders in Chapter 5 form the starting points for the SR policy of organisations, the SR core subjects and issues provide the content, or heart, of the SR guideline. This does not mean, however, that the core subjects and issues give a complete and exhaustive overview of *all* SR impact areas. Rather, they form an initial overview of impact areas that are, to some extent, relevant to all organisations.

This chapter begins with an introduction to the SR core subjects and issues, along with a few observations about the (im)possibilities of their applicability for organisations. Attention is given to several clarifications that the guideline provides to users. Next, we look at how the core subjects and issues are organised within ISO 26000. The guideline gives a (often concise) description of each SR core subject and SR issue, and defines the principles, starting points, guidelines and international conventions they are founded on. This chapter gives a few examples of these, but focuses mainly on the guideline's actions and expectations for each SR issue. The *essence* of what is expected is described for every SR core subject and SR issue. Finally, as an introduction to

Chapter 7, a few remarks are made concerning the specific application of the SR core subjects and issues.

6.2 **SR core subjects and issues**

ISO 26000 distinguishes between SR core subjects and SR issues. These SR impact areas (this is the general term that is used in this book for core subjects and issues together plus any other SR core subjects that are not mentioned in ISO 26000 explicitly) offer an effective way for organisations to orient themselves on SR and determine their social responsibilities. They form the content—the heart—of SR, according to ISO 26000. The guideline lists seven SR core subjects:

1. Organisational governance

2. Human rights

3. Labour practices

4. The environment

5. Fair operating practices

6. Consumer issues

7. Community involvement and development

Within ISO 26000 these specific core subjects were chosen because they form a modern reflection of 'good practice' in the area of SR. 'Good practice', however, is subject to change: a good example today may not be good tomorrow. The development and evolution of SR continues to proceed apace. This is a dynamic subject and the guideline reflects this.[1] Having said that, the core subjects cover the most probable economic, environmental and social effects (the 3Ps: people, planet, profit) for which an organisation should take responsibility.

Still, even the inexperienced reader will notice that these are very general and broad topics. The SR core subjects can have a multitude of connections with all types of organisations in all imaginable sectors. On the other hand, some of these subjects will not be recognised as being of importance to all

---

1 'Views of good practice too will undoubtedly change in the future, and additional issues may come to be seen as important elements of social responsibility' (ISO 2010: 5).

types of organisations. A retailer specialising in French cuisine, for example, will probably wonder to what extent 'Organisational governance' and 'Human rights' are applicable to their company, stores and employees. Such a retailer might want to add a subject, such as animal welfare, to the list. But ISO 26000 claims that any of these seven core subjects have at least some relevance to every type of organisation. Arguments can be made in favour of this statement, given the general formulations that are used, but the claim could be criticised in the sense that unless organisations feel engaged with the nuts and bolts of the guideline, there may be a temptation for some to turn off, or even ignore it. According to the IISD (Perera 2008), the statement that all core subjects are relevant for all organisations doesn't hold (see Interlude II). This is especially true for organisations with 30 employees or fewer, who state that they cannot identify with all of the SR core subjects.

ISO 26000 emphasises that to be able to recognise the organisational relevance of SR core subjects and SR issues, it can be helpful to take a look at interactions with other organisations and stakeholders. Once an organisation takes account of the impact of its activities and decisions on groups such as its customers, suppliers, partners, competitors and local communities, the picture may well become clearer.

As it is, ISO 26000 challenges the user of the guideline to determine the significance of the SR core subjects for their own organisation and to complement these where necessary. These additional subjects might surface during a stakeholder consultation or peer review. Every organisation should determine which SR impact areas are relevant to it, and which are important enough to become part of the organisation's SR profile.[2] The way ISO 26000 is applied differs per organisation: smaller companies, for example, will apply it more informally than multinational enterprises. It is important for organisations to realise that SR is a dynamic and evolving subject that might change shape and content in time as societal concerns develop.[3]

---

2 Chapter 7 will discuss selecting SR priorities and will go into further detail on this.
3 'Recognising social responsibility is a continuous process. The potential impacts of decisions and activities should be determined and taken into account during the planning stage of new activities. Ongoing activities should be reviewed as necessary so that the organisation can be confident that its social responsibility is still being addressed and can determine whether additional issues need to be taken into account' (ISO 2010: 16).

6.2.1 SR issues

Apart from the SR core subject 'Organisational governance', SR issues are distinguished within the other six core subjects, varying from four issues within 'The environment' to eight within 'Human rights'. ISO 26000 contains a total of 36 SR issues. The issues can be used as initial guidance for making the core subjects organisation-specific. Although ISO 26000 contends that all core subjects have at least some relevance to all organisations, this does not apply for all the SR issues. The SR issues can also be interpreted in many ways, depending on the individual organisation. Nevertheless, the lack of SR issues within the core subject 'Organisational governance' does appear odd, since relevant SR issues could have been distinguished, such as agreements about remuneration and fees for executives, reward structures and severance pay (including the way in which these are determined). 'Organisational governance' is considered a special core subject within ISO 26000 because it is different in nature to the other core subjects.[4] 'Organisational governance', therefore, is considered within ISO 26000 as a condition under which organisations integrate social responsibility throughout the organisation.

When looking at the issues several observations can be made. First, the SR core subjects and issues overlap and complement each other in a number of ways. ISO 26000 asks organisations that want to apply the guideline to deal with the core subjects and issues as a whole rather than looking at them in isolation. Positive actions that are undertaken in a certain impact area should not be executed at the expense of negative performance in another impact area. Organisations should also avoid taking action that results in negative effects on stakeholders or the value chain of the organisation. This is an odd stance that is not generally seen as part of the mainstream view of (C)SR. A broadly accepted notion within SR is that pursuing the interests of one stakeholder could damage the interests of another. This causes tension or dilemmas in decision-making. ISO 26000 challenges organisations to assess every action or decision for its possible harmful effects on other impact areas, stakeholder interests and consequences for society. Even when an action or decision has a small negative effect or consequence, according to ISO 26000, it should not be taken; or at least its negative effects should be neutralised. In practice, of course, this will not always prove an easy goal to accomplish and may indeed be impossible. Organisations cannot be expected to oversee and measure the

---

4 '[T]he nature of organisational governance is somewhat different from the other core subjects. Effective organisational governance enables an organisation to take action on the other core subjects and issues and to implement the principles [. . .]' (ISO 2010: 20).

impact on *all* their stakeholders of *every* action or decision. An organisation that applies the guideline should, in our opinion not take this challenge too literally. Second, it should be reiterated that the SR core subjects and issues do not represent an exhaustive list. In addition, the order of the core subjects and their respective issues do not suggest an order of importance (for example, concerning the efforts required by an organisation). Every organisation can therefore determine its own order of importance and allocate priorities accordingly. Third, and in anticipation of the next section, a glance at the complete overview of core subjects and issues shows that ISO 26000 repeats some aspects of SR in different SR impact areas. Examples include health and safety, and economic aspects, such as the life-cycle of products and the value chain of an organisation (backwards and forwards, including both customers and suppliers).

6.2.2 Structure of core subjects and actions and expectations per issue

The presentation and explanation of SR core subjects within ISO 26000 follows a fixed structure which is described below. First, ISO 26000 defines the core subject and then describes how it might relate to an organisation in different contexts and how important it might be to different entities. Examples are given of real-life instances for most core subjects. Next, the core subject is placed in the context of SR and a connection is made with sustainable development. This is done by describing the (potential) sustainability impact of a core subject or the relationship of the subject with broader developments in society. Subsequently, principles and considerations are mentioned that apply to the core subject. Here, it is important to avoid confusion with the general principles of SR that are specified by ISO 26000 (see Chapter 4). Instead, specific, fundamental principles that form the foundation of a core subject are discussed and some kind of minimal level of achievement or point of departure for an organisation is outlined. One example is the 1944 ILO Declaration of Philadelphia which says that labour is neither a tradeable good nor a commodity. Another example is the polluter pays principle.

In spelling out the core subjects, ISO 26000 intends to provide organisations with background information, inspiration and guidance in formulating their social responsibilities. For example, the core subject 'Community involvement and development' suggests activities aimed at local economic development, programmes to improve education and skills, and activities aimed at conserving culture heritage. Moreover, the type of investment an organisation makes in a local community will depend on the type of community it is, and on the unique expertise, resources and capacity that the organisation has to offer.

After the principles and considerations, the different SR issues that can be found under the SR core subjects, are described. For each SR issue a description is given and the specific relationship of the issue to social responsibility is defined.

Finally, ISO 26000 specifies for each SR issue the actions and/or the expectations concerning the behaviour, methods and performance of the organisation with regard to the respective SR issues. This happens (mainly) through the use of bullet points under the 'Related actions and expectations'. These actions and expectations are based on, or derived from, international conventions (e.g. UN Convention on Elimination of All Forms of Discrimination Against Women), recommendations (e.g. ILO Minimum Age Recommendation), declarations (e.g. ILO Tripartite Declaration of Principles Concerning Multinational Enterprises and Social Policy), guidelines (e.g. OECD Guidelines on the Protection of Privacy and Transborder Flows of Personal Data), agreements (e.g. UN Framework Convention on Climate Change) and existing ISO standards (e.g. ISO 9001 and ISO 27001). Throughout the guideline a frame containing a clarification of the specific issue is used: for example, about the Millennium Goals of the UN (part of the 'Community involvement and development' core subject; see also Annex 4) or about the ISO standards 10001, 10002 and 10003 on customer satisfaction (part of the 'Consumer issues' core subject). The actions and expectations are, in general, in the form of advice or suggestions, which is in line with the voluntary nature of the guideline.[5]

In the following sections the SR core subjects and issues are described and illustrated with a real-life example. To improve readability, the actions that an organisation should undertake according to ISO 26000 and the expectations the guideline sets out for organisations are summarised per SR issue. A detailed overview of the different SR issues can be found in the guideline itself.

---

5 'This International Standard contains no requirements and therefore the word "shall", which indicates a requirement in ISO language, is not used. Recommendations use the word "should". In some countries, certain recommendations of ISO 26000 are incorporated into law, and are therefore legally required. The word "may" is used to indicate that something is permitted. The word "can" is used to indicate that something is possible, for example, that an organisation or individual is able to do something' (ISO 2010: ix).

6.3 **Organisational governance**

The guideline describes 'Organisational governance' as the system that organisations have in place to make, implement and monitor their decisions and activities based on their mission, vision and strategy. Obviously, the managers and directors who lead the organisation have a big influence on the way the governance system is set up and how it works. In practice, there will be a difference between large and small organisations and how these decision-making processes work. In the former they will be more formal, while in the latter they can be very informal. In relation to SR the governance system makes it possible to implement and monitor SR and the SR principles alongside the other strategic priorities of the organisation. So, 'Organisational governance' in ISO 26000 is both a means to an end and an end in itself.

Unlike the other core subjects, no SR issues are distinguished within this core subject. However, several actions and expectations are specified—or, more accurately, the guideline specifies what the decision-making processes and structures should enable an organisation to do. In essence, ISO 26000 advises organisations on how to enable its employees to act in line with the general SR principles identified by the guideline. The most important condition that must be met is that SR should be integrated into the way the organisation makes it decisions, both formally and informally (ISO 2010: 21).

Example...
Unibail-Rodamco

To guarantee organisational governance Unibail-Rodamco adopted a multiple governance structure, including a supervisory board and a management board. The former consists of two committees—the governance, nomination and remuneration committee and the audit committee—which monitor and audit the enterprise. Through internal control and risk management, examinations and sometimes independent research these committees supervise the activities of the management board in order to avoid or identify any misuse or conflict of interest associated with the activities and relations of the management board.[6]

6 Unibail-Rodamco 2009 Annual Report: 167-68.

6.4 **Human rights**

Human rights are the basic rights that every person has or should have. They include civil and political rights, freedom of expression, social and cultural rights, and the right to health and education. Within the SR core subject 'Human rights' the following eight issues are distinguished:

1. Due diligence

2. Human rights risk situations

3. Avoidance of complicity

4. Resolving grievances

5. Discrimination and vulnerable groups

6. Civil and political rights

7. Economic, social and cultural rights

8. Fundamental principles and rights at work

6.4.1 Due diligence

Due diligence concerns the idea that an organisation should do its utmost to minimise any form of risk resulting from the activities it undertakes. This can evidently be relevant in many organisational activities, but as part of the SR core subject 'Human rights' it relates to minimising the risks of human rights violations across the supply chain of the organisation, both upstream and downstream.

Example...
Adidas

In order to improve its reputation and operational efficiency Adidas has established standards regarding the workplace of suppliers. In order to do business with Adidas suppliers must adhere to these standards which avoid malpractice in the areas of human rights and environmental impact. Internal inspections by Adidas of suppliers' premises to monitor adherence to the Workplace Standards are frequently verified by independent audits.[7]

7 Adidas, 'Compliance-related risks'; adidas-group.corporate-publications. com/2010/gb/en/group-management-report-financial-review/risk-and-opportunity-report/compliance-related-risks.html, accessed 12 March 2011.

6.4.2 Human rights risk situations

An organisation should be extra careful of, and caring for, human rights when it finds itself in a situation in which there is potential for human rights violations. Examples are: conflict situations; working in areas of extreme political instability; dealing with corrupt regimes; or managing complex international supply chains. Of course, in these situations, due diligence also plays an important role.

Example...
Employers Consultative Association of Malawi

The Employers Consultative Association of Malawi is a Malawian cooperative which, together with the ILO, coordinates the project Employers Fight Against Child Labour in Commercial Agriculture. The project's main goal is to care for the interests of employers on all socio-economic subjects, such as HIV/Aids, gender issues and child labour.[8]

6.4.3 Avoidance of complicity

Complicity is about conscious and unconscious assistance in committing illegal acts by others that lead to negative effects on people, planet or society. Three levels of complicity are distinguished: direct, beneficial and silent complicity. Direct complicity concerns the conscious and wilful violation of human rights. Beneficial complicity is directed at human rights violations committed by someone else or another organisation, but from which the organisation benefits directly. Finally, silent complicity addresses not speaking up when systematic or continuous human rights violations are known to the organisation, but outside its direct sphere of influence. ISO 26000 does not only refer to complicity in the legal sense, but also cites involvement in activities that have a substantial negative effect on human rights of which the organisation was aware or should have been aware. One manifestation here would be in not confronting systematic or long-standing violations of human rights.

8 ECAM, 'Employers fight against child labour project'; www.ilo.org/public/english/dialogue/actemp/downloads/projects/malawi_leaflet_en.pdf, accessed 23 March 2011.

Example...

The Ogoni people

The Ogoni people in Nigeria have been subject to many human rights viola-tions over the years. Their community is located in the Niger Delta, an area where Shell, and also Mobil, Chevron and Texaco, are responsible for oil spills and pollution. The Ogoni people have held many protests over the years, some of which were violently suppressed by the Nigerian police force, resulting in thousands of deaths and displacements. As Nigeria derives more than 80% of its revenues from the oil companies, it is in the government's interest to protect the oil companies' pipelines. However, when human rights violations result from these actions, it is the social responsibility of the oil companies to address these human rights violations and seek to prevent them.[9]

6.4.4 Resolving grievances

Whenever an organisation violates any of the human rights as identified in the International Bill of Human Rights, it should have an accessible and fair method in place to be called to account. In addition, the organisation should have a mechanism in place to resolve grievances and, when applicable, com-pensate the person or people involved (ISO 2010: 27).

Example...

Holy Rosary School

The Holy Rosary School is a private co-educational school in Victoria, Aus-tralia. To ensure just and equal relationships based on dignity between all the people related to the school, a grievance resolution policy and procedure has been drafted. The aim of this grievance resolution is:

- To provide a harmonious, positive and productive school environment.
- To resolve grievances fairly, efficiently and in accordance with require-ments and in a timely and effective manner.
- To have a sound and fair basis of information dissemination, conciliation, investigation and decision-making, which involve the principles of due process and natural justice.[10]

---

9 'Worldwide Shell Boycott. Shell Oil; Nigeria executes Niger Delta environmental protester/writer Ken Saro-Wiwa and 8 others'; findarticles.com/p/articles/mi_m1295/is_n1_v60/ai_17963624, accessed 23 March 2011.

10 'Holy Rosary School: Grievance Resolution Policy and Procedure'; www.holyrosary.tas.edu.au/documents/GRIEVANCERESOLUTIONPOLICY.pdf, accessed 23 March 2011.

6.4.5 Discrimination and vulnerable groups

Discrimination concerns making a distinction, exclusion or having a preference that leads to the unequal treatment of a person or group, or it concerns a situation where there is no universal access to equal opportunities. Discrimination is one of the most serious violations of human rights. It is the responsibility of every organisation to act in such a way that it does not discriminate against any of its stakeholders, directly or indirectly, now or in the future.

An organisation should take particular care not to discriminate against key vulnerable groups, such as women (equal treatment in the economic, social and political sense is the starting point), people with a disability (for example, by offering integration, participation or adapted facilities), children (respecting their right to life, survival and development), local communities, migrants and migrant workers, and others (for example, people without a caste). ISO 26000 also states that an organisation should make an effort to improve situations that are the consequences of discrimination in the past.

Did you know...

Research from the University of Groningen shows that the percentage of women in the higher echelons of government mainly increases because men leave for positions with more status and not because of a successful recruitment or promotion policy.[11]

Example...
Dutch Ministry of Public Health, Wellbeing and Sport
The Dutch Ministry of Public Health, Wellbeing and Sport has developed a policy to have people with a disability participate in the labour process and society in the same way as people without a disability. The Ministry encourages all government departments to make specific arrangements to make the policy successful.

---

11 University of Groningen, 'Rijksoverheid feminiseert: vooral mannen in hogere functies verlaten de dienst', 3 August 2009; www.rug.nl/corporate/nieuws/archief/archief2009/persberichten/116_09, accessed 16 March 2011.

6.4.6 Civil and political rights

This SR issue is specifically about having rights and liberties including the right to safety, the right to a life with dignity, the right to have possessions and freedom of religion. Organisations should respect these rights.

Example...

Tesco

Under strict Sharia law, Muslims are not allowed to carry alcohol. In order to respect the freedom of religion and to avoid any problems, Tesco has introduced into its induction process for shelf stockers and other store personnel the forewarning that handling of alcohol is part of the job. If employees object to handling alcohol on religious grounds, Tesco has an open-door policy for staff to discuss such issues.[12]

6.4.7 Economic, social and cultural rights

Every organisation should acknowledge that every person is a member of society and therefore has a right to education, health, a standard of living that is beneficial to their health and the well-being of themselves and their family. This includes food, clothing, housing, medical care and social securities. An organisation should respect these economic, social and cultural rights, in the context of the local situation, and assess the impact of its activities, products and services on these rights.[13] This issue also relates to content in the core subject 'Community involvement and development' (see §6.9).

12 David Wilkes, 'Devout Muslim sues Tesco for making him carry alcohol', *Daily Mail*, 29 September 2008; www.dailymail.co.uk/news/article-1063590/Devout-Muslim-sues-Tesco-making-carry-alcohol.html, accessed 23 March 2011.

13 ISO 26000 gives, among others, the following example to illustrate the kind of activity or initiative an organisation should not take (ISO 2010: 30): '[I]t should neither directly, nor indirectly limit nor deny access to an essential product or resource, such as water.'

Example...

Heineken

Heineken has produced an 'economic impact assessment model' dealing with the daily business operations of one of its factories in Sierra Leone. The model identifies ways of decreasing the negative impacts of the company's activities. Its main objective, however, is to increase positive impacts by, especially, helping local communities improve their economic and social situations.[14]

6.4.8 Fundamental principles and rights at work

Despite the firm legal grounds of many of these rights in the developed world, organisations should still take care to pay attention to freedom of (labour) association and collective negotiation (for example, offering suitable facilities and access to information and resources to people that hold a representative position to resolve differences), forced labour/slavery, equal opportunities and non-discrimination (for example, the prevention of sexual harassment) and child labour. The guideline states that an organisation should undertake a periodic overview of the effects of policies aimed at increasing equal opportunities and non-discriminatory practices, and take action to stimulate the protection and improvement of the situation of vulnerable groups (ISO 2010: 31-32).

Example...

Google

Google is covering a cost that gay and lesbian employees have to pay when their partners receive domestic partner health benefits. Due to US tax laws, domestic partners that are not married pay around a $1,000 more annually for healthcare services. This extra cost can be avoided by heterosexual couples if they choose to get married (the federal government of the United States does not recognise the marriages of same-sex couples). Google is not the first company to cover these expenses; Cisco, Kimpton Hotels and the Gates Foundation have already implemented similar policies.[15]

---

14 www.ncdo.nl/docs/uploads/Onderzoek20.pdf, accessed 25 April 2011.
15 Tara Siegel Bernard, 'Google to add pay to cover a tax for same-sex benefits', *New York Times*, 30 June 2010; www.nytimes.com/2010/07/01/your-money/01benefits. html?_r=1, accessed 23 March 2011.

6.5 **Labour practices**

The SR core subject 'Labour practices' applies to all the policies and activities related to work that are done within, by or on behalf of an organisation. It is therefore not only relevant for employees but also to work undertaken by the organisation on the premises of others or work that is done in the name of the organisation by subcontractors or third parties.

Within the SR core subject 'Labour practices' the following five issues are distinguished:

1. Employment and employment relationships

2. Conditions of work and social protection

3. Social dialogue

4. Health and safety at work

5. Human development and training in the workplace

6.5.1 Employment and employment relationships

The focus here is on the importance of employment for human development. The provision of employment is one of the main contributions to a decent standard of living. In this respect an organisation, as employer, has the responsibility to contribute to a certain amount of stability with regard to the quality of life of its employees by offering job security and at least a minimum income. From this point of view, both employers as well as employees have certain rights and obligations towards one another and, in some regards, also towards society as a whole. This SR issue has, in contrast to the SR core subject in general, no relation to subcontractors and the services of third parties.

Example...
Business Link

The British advisory and support service for companies, Business Link, offers a manual for companies with the title 'How to Dismiss Employees Correctly'. This is an online tool that can be used to go through the correct dismissal procedure. In addition, the instrument contains a summary of the progress of an employer in the dismissal procedure, advice and reference to complementing information.

6.5.2 Conditions of work and social protection

ISO 26000 identifies different basic norms regarding working conditions and social protection. There are many aspects contributing to decent working conditions, such as a work–life balance, paid leave, a certain minimum wage, compensation for overtime and the minimum standards as set out by the ILO. The issue of working conditions and the degree of social protection available are particularly (though not exclusively) important in situations and countries where the law is silent. Therefore, this part of the SR guideline applies especially to organisations (including those that have production activities or part of their supply chain) in developing countries.

Example...

Marks & Spencer

In 2007 Marks & Spencer launched Plan A, which contains 100 commitments to climate change, waste, natural resources, fair partnering, and health and wellbeing. Part of the aim of Plan A is to ensure good working conditions in the supply chain. To achieve this, Marks & Spencer has, as well as setting criteria for its suppliers and buying Fairtrade-certified cotton, set up 10 'Ethical Model Factories' to demonstrate that good working conditions improve the productivity of the workforce.[16]

6.5.3 Social dialogue

The concept of social dialogue, as ISO 26000 describes it, is derived from the definition that the ILO uses as, 'all types of negotiation, consultation or simply exchange of information between, or among, representatives of governments, employers and workers, on issues of common interest relating to economic and social policy.'[17] Where the SR issue 'Fundamental principles and rights in the workplace' concerns expectations associated with freedom of association and collective negotiation, social dialogue is about the way content is determined at an individual, industry, national or international level. In Europe, this process concerns mainly the development of collective labour

---

16 M&S, 'How We Do Business Report 2010'; plana.marksandspencer.com/media/pdf/planA-2010.pdf, accessed 23 March 2011.
17 ILO, 'Social Dialogue'; www.ilo.org/public/english/dialogue/ifpdial/areas/social.htm, accessed 16 March 2011.

agreements, as well as how governments, employers and employees deal with topics that are part of these agreements.

Example...
ConocoPhillips

At ConocoPhillips a continuous dialogue with employees takes place. The goal is to gain insight into the opinions of employees and their view of the company. This is done in different ways: for example, through surveys to collect the opinions of employees, internet forums, assessments of the company by employees and direct meetings with employees. Because of the great diversity of employees the research is conducted in 16 languages.[18]

6.5.4 Health and safety at work

The SR issue 'Health and safety at work' concerns not only the physical, but also the psychological and social aspects of work. It is the responsibility of the employer to make sure that working conditions do not cause discomfort or harm. It should be noted that in some cases where working conditions are poor, it is not only the employee's health at stake, but also the environment with potential impacts on local communities or even society as a whole. A good example in this respect is working with toxic or highly explosive materials. For the relationship between health and safety at work and the environment see also the SR core subject 'The environment'.

Example...
Burando Maritime Services

Burando Maritime Services offers a wide range of services to vessels visiting the Port of Rotterdam, including, among other things, fuel oil. The company has drawn up safety conditions for transporting and working with fuel oil. These prescriptions describe the associated dangers, what should be done to limit risk and how employees should handle accidents.

18 ConocoPhilips, 'Supporting Employee Dialogue'; www.cpcsustainability.com/canada-wide-issues/social/cwiemployees/employees-dialogue.cfm, accessed 23 March 2011.

6.5.5 Human development and training in the workplace

The SR issue 'Employment and employment relationships' makes a case for secure employment contributing to quality of life. But it is not only through the provision of job security and a decent wage that employers can contribute to their workers' quality of life. Through training and human development employees can increase their capacities and competencies which, in turn, broaden their horizons and increase their chances of a promotion or a better job. Furthermore, ISO 26000 states that human development can also improve workers' access to political, economic and social opportunities, ability to contribute to society as a whole and feelings of self-worth (ISO 2010: 40).

Example...
Sainsbury's

In one of their stores in Camden, north London, a Sainsbury's bakery team has developed a flexible system consisting of a number of different baking shifts throughout the day. All team members have agreed to rotate their hours each week to make sure that no employees worked a shift that did not match their personal life.[19]

6.6 **The environment**

Every society has an ecological footprint as does every organisation. Problems occur when this footprint is larger than the environment can bear. Current crises, such as on energy, food, water, climate and biodiversity, are all believed to be (at least, in part) caused by humans. Organisations play a role in terms of their contribution to these problems. However, they also have a role to play in solving them by reducing their ecological footprint. This requires an extensive and systematic approach that includes cooperation with other organisations.

Did you know...

The production of one kilo of steak requires on average 16,000 litres of water.[20]

19 J. Sainsbury plc, 'Equality, Diversity and Inclusion'; www.j-sainsbury.co.uk/cr09/index.asp?pageid=53, accessed 23 March 2011.
20 Water Footprint Network, www.waterfootprint.org, accessed 16 March 2011.

Within the SR core subject 'The environment' four SR issues are distinguished:

1. Prevention of pollution

2. Sustainable resource use

3. Climate change mitigation and adaptation

4. Protection of the environment and restoration of natural habitats

It should be noted that the term 'environment' within this SR core subject relates to wildlife as well as to habitats and ecosystems.

6.6.1 Prevention of pollution

In essence, pollution comes down to the introduction of contaminants into the environment. These contaminants can take many forms, including the dumping of toxic materials, the release of polluted emissions to air, contaminated discharges to water and noise from an organisation's activities. Organisations should aim to avoid these and other types of pollution.

Example...
The city of Nieuwegein
The city of Nieuwegein in the Netherlands makes agreements with partners and takes environmentally friendly actions to reduce its ecological footprint. Together, these agreements and actions, in the areas of energy, lighting, warmth, cleaning, sanitation, pesticide use and chemical waste, are managed by an ISO 14001 environmental management system.[21]

6.6.2 Sustainable resource use

Current consumption and production patterns are not sustainable. Society takes more from the environment than the carrying capacity of the planet can withstand. Therefore people and organisations should use resources more sustainably, which means that natural resources should be consumed at a pace slower than or equal to the ability of the Earth can renew this resource. ISO 26000 identifies three areas for improvement: energy efficiency; conservation of and access to water; and efficiency in the use of materials.

21 Gemeente Nieuwegein, 'Interne Milieuzorg'; www.nieuwegein.nl/infotype/webpage/view.asp?objectID=3509, accessed 23 March 2011.

Example...
Kimberly-Clark

To conserve forests Kimberly-Clark has improved its procurement standards together with Greenpeace. By the end of 2011 Kimberly-Clark strives to procure at least 40% of its North American tissue fibre from FSC-certified or recycled sources.[22]

6.6.3 Climate change mitigation and adaptation

Climate change is one the largest environmental problems of our time. Consequences of climate change are likely to include higher temperatures, melting ice and therefore higher sea levels, but also more frequent extreme weather events and increased ecosystem disruption. The related actions and expectations for organisations specified by ISO 26000 are divided between 'Climate change mitigation' and 'Climate change adaptation'. The first category concerns reducing the effects of organisations on the climate, while the second relates to the ability of organisations to adapt to the consequences of climate change. The intention here is to enable an organisation to limit its vulnerability to the results of climate change.

Example...
Water authority Vallei & Eem

Water authority Vallei & Eem in the Netherlands is preparing itself for a likely warmer and more unpredictable climate with more rain within shorter periods and longer periods of drought. This requires necessary adaptations in the regional water management strategy. This strategy deals mainly with protection against floods, water shortages, drought and maintaining water quality and ecology.

---

22 Forest Stewardship Council, 'Kimberly-Clark sets preference for FSC in revised procurement policy', 12 August 2009; www.fsc.org/news.html?&no_cache=1&tx_ ttnews%5Btt_news%5D=176&cHash=c3ece6fa5d, accessed 16 March 2011.

6.6.4 Protection of the environment and restoration of natural habitats

Within this SR issue the focus is mainly on the influence of human activities on ecosystems. The increasing demand for natural resources caused by societal overconsumption has a big impact on ecosystems—species disappear, natural habitats diminish and, as a consequence, biodiversity decreases.

Did you know...

At present rates, natural forests in Indonesia would be logged out within 10 years, Papua New Guinea within 13–16 years.[23]

The four most important areas within this issue are: valuing, protecting and restoring ecosystems; valuing and protecting biodiversity; using land and natural resources sustainably; and advancing environmentally sound urban and rural development (ISO 2010: 46-47).

6.7 **Fair operating practices**

This SR core subject concerns the way organisations act towards, and interact with, their stakeholders. These stakeholders can be individuals as well as other organisations such as suppliers, governments or business partners. The interaction of the organisation with these stakeholders should be based on the principles of ethical behaviour. Within the core subject 'Fair operating practices' the following five SR issues are distinguished:

1. Anti-corruption

2. Responsible political involvement

3. Fair competition

4. Promoting social responsibility in the value chain

5. Respect for property rights

---

23 Andy White, Xiufang Sun, Kerstin Canby, Jintao Xu, Christopher Barr, Eugenia Katsigris, Gary Bull, Christian Cossalter, Sten Nilsson, *China and the Global Market for Forest Products: Transforming Trade to Benefit Forests and Livelihoods* (Forest Trends, Center for Chinese Agricultural Policy [CIFOR], 2006): 13.

6.7.1 **Anti-corruption**

Under no circumstances should any organisation engage in activities that are related to corruption, directly or indirectly. Apart from the immoral nature of corruption, ISO 26000 identifies several risks for organisations engaging in such practices that might undermine their reputation or result in legal consequences such as criminal prosecution. Furthermore, corruption is highly likely to result in social disparities, such as unfair competition or an unequal distribution of wealth. Corruption can take many forms such as bribery of public officials, bribery in the private sector, fraud and money laundering.

Example...
Transparency International

The corruption index of Transparency International measures the perceived levels of corruption in the public sector of all countries around the world. The results for 2010 show that Denmark, New Zealand and Singapore are perceived as least corrupt, while Somalia is perceived as the most corrupt country.[24]

6.7.2 **Responsible political involvement**

Organisations should avoid undue involvement in public political processes and not seek to exert excessive influence over them. While ISO 26000 does not suggest that there should be no involvement (where this is appropriate) it is clearly stated that the extent should be limited and organisations should refrain from undermining the political process or becoming involved in bribery, manipulation or intimidation. Furthermore, it is suggested that organisations should at least be transparent about their activities or policies regarding lobbying, but also political contributions and involvement. It looks like the organisational stakeholders in the process of developing the guideline did not dare to say too much about lobbying. Nevertheless, the SR issue is about setting the boundaries of, or at least being transparent about, the political involvement of organisations.

24 Transparency International, 'Corruption Perceptions Index 2010 Results'; www. transparency.org/policy_research/surveys_indices/cpi/2010/results, accessed 23 March 2011.

Example...
Procter & Gamble

Procter & Gamble makes clear on its website in which ways the organisation is involved in politics. The lobbying and political activities of the company are explained and there is a commission that is responsible for this. In addition, the amount of money related to these activities is specified.

6.7.3 Fair competition

ISO 26000 states that fair and open competition creates a wide range of (societal) benefits. These range from providing a stimulus to innovate to a level playing field for economic growth; and from producing cheaper products and services to higher quality. Some examples of anti-competitive behaviour that should be avoided are price fixing, forming cartels and underselling in order to drive competitors out of the market.

Example...
Toshiba

The Toshiba Group Policy states that Toshiba will not engage in unfair competition. To ensure that their employees promote fair competition Toshiba has implemented competition law compliance programmes for local employees. Furthermore, specific rules for marketing and sales have been developed and implemented, such as the avoidance of the allocation of markets and agreements on pricing. These rules are not only related to written, but also oral agreements.[25]

6.7.4 Promoting social responsibility in the value chain

Within a free-market relationship one organisation can exert influence on other organisations: for example, through procurement and tendering. By using its influence in the supply chain a powerful organisation can promote (or demand) the adoption of SR principles and methods by its suppliers and by their suppliers. The upshot could be the adoption of more sustainable practices throughout the supply chain of the organisation, or, at the very least, the minimisation of negative practices or impacts.

25 'Toshiba Group Standards of Conduct: 4. Procurement'; www.toshiba.co.jp/csr/en/policy/soc.htm - SOC01_4, accessed 23 March 2011.

Example...
The city of Amsterdam

The city of Amsterdam includes sustainability as a criteria at every level of its procurement strategy. The city's 'Guideline on Sustainable Purchasing' assists its procurement officers to take sustainability issues into account when selecting tenders. For every step of the procurement process, possible considerations and questions are asked, including: 'What things can you demand from a supplier and how should you formulate those demands?' and 'How can you challenge the market to come up with innovative solutions?'

6.7.5 Respect for property rights

When organisations and individuals know that their property rights are respected, they are more likely to invest in innovation, property development and, therefore, social and economic security. Property rights involve both physical and intellectual property, such as copyright, patents and moral rights (ISO 2010: 51). Every organisation should respect these rights.

Example...
Business Software Alliance

To prevent dissemination and halt the use of illegal software by organisations, software and hardware companies such as Siemens, Adobe, Apple and Symantec have founded the international Business Software Alliance. This non-profit organisation has a mission to promote the conditions under which the information technology industry can thrive and continue to develop its products.[26]

6.8 **Consumer issues**

The focus here is on the individual. People, as well as organisations, can contribute to sustainable development in the way they lead their lives and undertake their daily activities. So, organisations that produce or supply

26 Business Software Alliance, 'About BSA & Members'; www.bsa.org/country/BSA and Members.aspx, accessed 23 March 2011.

consumer products and services should inform buyers about the sustainability attributes of their offerings throughout the life-cycle: from usage to disposal. Within the SR core subject 'Consumer issues' the following seven SR issues are discussed:

1. Fair marketing, information and contractual practices

2. Protecting consumers' health and safety

3. Sustainable consumption

4. Consumer service, support and dispute resolution

5. Consumer data protection and privacy

6. Access to essential services

7. Education and awareness

6.8.1 Fair marketing, factual and unbiased information and fair contractual practices

This SR issue includes, among other things, allowing consumers to accurately compare the characteristics of products and services and so make informed decisions in the purchasing process. Key elements of responsible marketing practice should be to provide consumers with information on the sustainability impact of a product. This should include declarations on its journey through the supply chain and on the full life-cycle of the product.

Did you know . . .

An increasing number of initiatives can be seen that aim to highlight the practice of 'greenwashing' by large companies in commercials, marketing efforts and press statements. In the United States Greenpeace has initiated the Stopgreenwash.org project, one of its many efforts to combat greenwashing.[27]

The organisation that sells products to the end consumer does not always possess all of the relevant information that consumers need to make an educated decision. Therefore, it is also the responsibility of the supplier to provide its customers with full and detailed information on the sustainability impacts of its product. Finally this SR issue also zooms in on a balanced power distribution in the (negotiation) relationships in the whole chain. In this respect, the guideline advises that the parties with high negotiation power do not include unfair terms in their contracts, such as the provision to make unilateral

27 Greenpeace, 'Greenwashing: History'; www.stopgreenwash.org/history, accessed 23 March 2011.

changes in the contract, or entering into contracts with unreasonably long contract periods.

Example...
Borrowing money costs money

Since 1 April 2009 the AFM, the Dutch Authority Financial Markets, on behalf of the Dutch government, requires financial companies to add a warning to their advertising about credit, highlighting the possible consequences of taking such credit. The goal of this warning is to increase the awareness of consumers about the consequences of borrowing money. The warning phrase is: 'Pay attention! Borrowing money costs money.'

6.8.2 Protection of consumers' health and safety

Regarding this SR issue, ISO 26000 states that organisations should pay special attention to groups that are more vulnerable, such as children, who are usually not able to identify the potential dangers from using certain products. Therefore, products and services have to be safe to such a degree that, during normal usage, or in situations in which possible abuse can be foreseen, they do not damage consumers' health. Consequently, it is important that an organisation goes beyond laws and regulations regarding safety requirements. Of course, even when all preventative measures have been taken, it is still possible that an unforeseen fault or danger comes to light through consumer usage. In that case, organisations should have a mechanism in place to recall the product.

Example...
ECOstyle

ECOstyle is a Dutch company that produces and sells environmentally friendly plant protection, fertilisers and pesticides throughout Europe. Since no chemicals or damaging substances are used, the gardens in which children and domestic pets play becomes a safer environment with lower health risks.[28]

28 www.ecostyle.nl

6.8.3 Sustainable consumption

At the famous UN Conference on Environment and Development in Rio de Janeiro in 1992 sustainable consumption and production was recognised as an important concept to link environment and development challenges. Two years later, at the Oslo Symposium, the following definition of sustainable consumption was agreed upon: 'the use of services and related products which respond to basic needs [. . .] so as not to jeopardise the needs of future generations'.[29] Current Western patterns of consumption are largely not sustainable.

Did you know...

The carbon footprint of a trip from Europe to Australia or Oceania is 13 times as large as that of an average holiday by car within Europe.[30]

Purchasing a product or service impacts on sustainable development. Organisations have a responsibility to make consumers aware of the arguments for sustainable consumption in order to allow them to make informed decisions about their purchases and choose a more sustainable lifestyle.

Example...
Starbucks

From March 2010 all Starbucks stores throughout Europe have been selling 100% Fairtrade-certified coffee. This coffee is purchased from producers that produce coffee in a responsible and sustainable way. Starbucks goes further, however: it also educates its customers about the meaning of Fairtrade coffee via in-store posters and flyers.[31]

6.8.4 Consumer service, support and dispute resolution

This issue concerns after-sales service and the way the organisation provides for the needs of consumers after a sale of a product or service has taken place. So, topics such as the sales warranty, technical support available during usage,

---

29 UNEP, 'What is Sustainable Consumption and Production (SCP)?'; www.rona.unep. org/about_unep_rona/SCP/index.html, accessed 16 March 2011.

30 De Bruin, K., R. Dirven, E. Eijgelaar and P. Peeters, *Reizen op grote voet 2008: De carbon footprint van vakanties van Nederlanders in 2008 en ontwikkelingen sinds 2002* (Kenniscentrum [Kust]toerisme, 2008): 18

31 'Starbucks fairtrade coffee', 6 March 2010; www.goodsense.nu/2010/03/06/4242 and 'Responsibly Grown Coffee'; www.starbucks.com/responsibility/sourcing/ coffee, accessed 23 March 2011.

conditions for returning products and procedures for dealing fairly with complaints and resolving disputes are included here.

Example...
Technocash

Technocash is a company that focuses on money transfers for both companies and individuals. The company has a policy for dealing with complaints and resolving disputes. This policy is about the process of settling complaints and solving disputes, and clear communication about these processes towards clients is a central part of the policy.[32]

6.8.5 Consumer data protection and privacy

We live in a world where information can be gathered and disseminated rapidly and globally. However, modern technologies also mean that consumers run a greater risk of having their privacy compromised. It is the responsibility of an organisation to ensure that this privacy is respected, which in turn can boost consumer trust in an organisation as well as its reputation and credibility.

Example...
UNICEF

Several UNICEF websites are aimed at raising awareness about the living conditions of children in developing countries and encourage schoolchildren from developed countries to participate in programmes to improve these living conditions. Some of these websites contain interactive elements, such as discussion forums. To prevent abuse, UNICEF asks for detailed information from site users, and children are encouraged to inform their parents about their use of these websites.

6.8.6 Access to essential services

Organisations that supply essential services, such as gas, electricity, water and sewerage, have a special responsibility, according to ISO 26000. Only in exceptional circumstances may these services be withdrawn, and utilities

32 www.technocash.com

providers need to adopt clear policies on, for example, late payment of bills by customers.

Example...
Guidelines on shutting down electricity and gas of small households

According to a 2006 guideline of the Dutch Ministry of Economic Affairs a company that transports or supplies electricity or gas to small households is not allowed to shut off supply to a household in the period between 1 October to 1 April of any year, unless the household requests the company to do so, commits fraud or misuse, there is a safety issue, or there is no known bill holder at the household with a connection to the service network. Late payment by a household, is not, therefore, a reason to withhold these essential services.

6.8.7 Education and awareness

Not all consumers are aware of their rights and responsibilities, nor are they aware of all of the impacts of the products and services they buy. It is, in part, the responsibility of organisations to raise this awareness and provide information in order for consumers to make more informed purchasing decisions and to exercise their rights and responsibilities.

Example...
AH puur&eerlijk

AH (Albert Heijn), the largest Dutch chain of supermarkets, has developed a new sustainability brand of its own: AH puur&eerlijk (pure&fair). As a recognisable brand AH offers a range of responsible products produced, grown or procured with extra care for people, animals, nature or the environment. The products of AH puur&eerlijk always have either an independent eco-label such as the EKO label for biological products or a third-party label of an independent NGO.

6.9 Community involvement and development

The relationship between organisations and their (local) environment or communities is an integral part of their social responsibilities. The goal for organisations in community engagement is to contribute to the social, economic and political development of the communities they operate in, either in developed, developing or underdeveloped countries. For the most part the contributions made in developing and underdeveloped countries might have a more significant impact; however, the organisation should always look at its local community and try to find the relationship with its own activities and employees' wishes. This contribution should stem from the fact that organisations recognises that it, as well as the communities in which it operates, is part of society as a whole and that it therefore shares certain interests. Philanthropy alone, according to ISO 26000, cannot be seen as a substitute for other forms of community engagement that are described under this SR issue. Still, philanthropy is seen by the guideline as one form of social or community investment. Within the SR core subject 'Community involvement and development' the following seven SR issues are distinguished:

1. Community involvement

2. Education and culture

3. Employment creation and skills development

4. Technology development and access

5. Wealth and income creation

6. Health

7. Social investment

6.9.1 Community involvement

In essence, community involvement concerns an organisation's contribution to society beyond the impacts of its day-to-day business. This contribution can take many forms, such as donations in kind, partnerships with local groups, shared opportunities for positive exposure and enabling employees to help in solving or preventing a local social problem. Through community involvement an organisation builds bonds, and also gets a better understanding of the issues relevant to the communities it operates in. This improved cooperation with the community may lead to a process of joint development or co-evolution, but also creates opportunities for members of the community to participate in the decision-making processes of the organisation.

Example...

Albron

The so-called MaStafette is an initiative of Fortis Foundation to offer high-school students the possibility of undertaking a social internship. Students make a pro bono contribution to society: for example, in care for the elderly, education or for other good causes. Albron, a Dutch caterer, participates in this project, coaching the students, and students perform their internships with the company working with groups and parts of society they would not otherwise interact with in order to enhance their learning experience.[33]

6.9.2 Education and culture

For communities to thrive while preserving their own identity and culture, it is important that they enjoy proper education which in turn strengthens social cohesion. Obviously, this issue is linked to underdeveloped and developing countries, and rightly so, since the state does not always provide the best education. However, reducing the illiteracy rate in developed countries, for instance as part of a employee development programme, is also an aspect that is covered by this issue.

Example...

MeesterMatch

MeesterMatch, a personnel recruitment and selection company, participates in the One Laptop Per Child programme. Participating in this initiative means that the organisation donates one laptop to a child in a developing country for every successful match made between an employer and a candidate by their company. Through this programme, MeesterMatch hopes to contribute to reducing the knowledge gap in developing countries.[34]

---

33 'Albron sponsort prijs Beste Stagebieder'; www.nov.nl/smartsite.dws?id=129348, accessed 27 April 2011.
34 'Onderwijs OLPC en MeesterMatch helpen kinderen in ontwikkelingslanden'; www.nieuwsbank.nl/inp/2009/03/06/A004.htm, accessed 27 April 2011

6.9.3 Employment creation and skills development

Both creating employment and developing skills contributes to the economic and social development of communities and society. By providing these social goods, organisations contribute to reducing poverty and help people to ensure that they have the skills or qualifications for a decent and productive job.

Example...
Pilbara

The Australian logistics company Pilbara operates in remote areas. There are relatively few chances of getting educated or employed for the local citizens. Half of Pilbara's employees come from the local community. This is a conscious choice by Pilbara. Working is a socialisation process for employees and their families. The company offers its employees a social structure and the opportunity of participating more actively in the community because of their increased standard of living. Additionally, the knowledge and experience they acquire makes it easier for local community members to find employment after a Pilbara project has ended.[35]

6.9.4 Technology development and access

Clearly, there are many economic and social benefits associated with having access to modern technologies. Organisations can contribute to bridging the so-called 'digital divide' by supplying communities with access to information and technology.

Example...
Close the Gap

Close the Gap is an international non-profit organisation with a mission to close the digital divide. The organisation does this by making high quality and cost-efficient ICT equipment available to educational projects in developing countries. The organisation cooperates with companies such as Ricoh, Cisco and KLM.[36]

35 www.pilbaralogistics.com.au
36 www.close-the-gap.org

6.9.5 Wealth and income creation

According to ISO 26000, entrepreneurship is promulgated as a force for good that can benefit the structural development of a community and reduce poverty. There are many possibilities for organisations to make a contribution to a climate where entrepreneurship is stimulated: for example, by steering procurement towards local suppliers and recruiting managers from the local population. Furthermore, this SR issue concerns the fairer distribution of wealth—something that organisations can also contribute to.

6.9.6 Health

Good health is a prerequisite for the economic and social development of a community. Organisations can contribute by promoting awareness about health issues and by providing health services to employees and their family members where appropriate.

Example...
Nike

The headquarters of Nike in the Netherlands has been designed with the health of employees in mind. Workers have a football and basketball court at their disposal, as well as an indoor sports facility and a gym, an athletics track and two tennis courts. All of this is offered for free. Yoga classes are offered for just a few euros. The goal is to encourage healthy employees who can contribute productively to the company while enjoying a better quality of life in general.

6.9.7 Social investment

Organisations can contribute to human development and create socially stable societies through projects in the areas of education, culture and healthcare. Such social investments should take place with the participation of local communities as they are in the best position to make sure that attention and efforts focus on the right issues and priorities.

Example...

Netcare

Netcare Group is a South African organisation comprising many hospitals and other healthcare institutions. Netcare has developed a Corporate Social Investment Policy with which it makes a contribution to socio-economic development in South Africa. Most activities and investments that stem from this policy are related to healthcare, such as pre-hospital emergency medical services.[37]

6.10 **Final words**

A quick look at the 'requirements' of ISO 26000 could potentially discourage an organisation to use the guideline as the basis for its policy on social responsibility. Possible criticism is obvious. The SR core subjects and issues that are detailed within ISO 26000, and the manner in which they have been formulated, can be perceived as being overly ambitious. The content of ISO 26000 focuses rather generally on solving urgent global problems, such as poverty, climate change, human rights violations, to contribute towards a sustainable world and asks organisations for wide-ranging commitments to this end. In addition, the guideline seems to have been drawn up with large internationally operating companies in mind. Many of the SR issues could be seen as irrelevant for SMEs that do not have production activities abroad or import from developing countries. The relevance for local governments in developed countries is also hard to fathom. It is no surprise that research by the IISD (Perera 2008) has shown that the majority of respondents thought that ISO 26000 was not suitable for SMEs, nor for other organisations apart from multinationals.

Still, the aim here was for a guideline on social responsibility that contributes towards sustainable development. SR issues, such as stopping child labour, avoiding the depletion of natural resources, stamping out inhumane working conditions, protecting vulnerable groups and ensuring the health and safety of employees and consumers, are some of the most important areas for sustainable development.

Many of these issues have currency outside the world of the multinational. Care for employees, equal treatment of men and women, limiting carbon

37 www.netcare.co.za/live/netcare_content.php?Item_ID=5402&Revision=en/5, accessed 27 April 2011.

emissions, applying sustainability criteria in procurement processes, operating with integrity, community involvement, fair dealings with consumers—these are areas that are as relevant to SMEs, governmental organisations and NGOs as to corporations.

ISO 26000 emphasises that the SR core subjects it specifies are, to a certain extent and in *some way*, relevant for every organisation. In this way, the SR core subjects offer a kind of foundation for sustainability—a minimum performance level that should be achieved at least for organisations that want to base their SR policy on ISO 26000.[38] This is different for the SR issues, however: these may well be irrelevant to some organisations.

The way the SR core subjects and issues apply to organisations depends on what type of organisation they are, the kind of activities they undertake, the products and/or services they offer, their stakeholders and the characteristics of the environment and communities within which they operate. The scope and the sphere of influence of one organisation may be completely different from that of another in the same sector, let alone a different *kind* of organisation. Additionally, the SR core subjects and the SR issues that are described in ISO 26000 do not in any way provide a complete or exhaustive overview of SR subject areas—there are many more SR themes that one can think of.

To make sure that the application of ISO 26000 covers as many types of organisations as possible, the guideline offers organisations room for manoeuvre in engaging with SR in their own way. An organisation should map its relevant and important SR topics and select its own SR priorities. One of the starting points for this is the concept of sustainability impact. Selecting SR priorities is the subject of the next chapter.

---

38 It is emphasised here that it is not the intention of ISO 26000 that organisations only fulfil these 'minimum requirements'. That would give ISO 26000 a compliance character: it is the goal of ISO 26000 to encourage organisations to fulfil their social responsibilities in a way that goes beyond the specifications in the guideline and to continually improve their SR performance.

Interlude V
The materiality of ISO 26000 for SMEs

V.1 Introduction

In 2008, the IISD (International Institute for Sustainable Development) conducted a study among SMEs and SME support organisations into the materiality of ISO 26000 for SMEs. One aspect of this study was a so-called materiality test of the principles and core subjects included in ISO 26000. The researchers' objective was to determine materiality from the perspective of the relevance of core subjects for stakeholder relationships and company profitability.

V.2 How material are the ISO 26000 principles for SMEs?

The IISD research showed that, according to SMEs, 'Respect for the rule of law' is seen as being the most material principle for company profitability (see Fig. V.1). 'Respect for stakeholder interests' was, not surprisingly, perceived as being most material for stakeholder relationships. However, 'Respect for international norms of behaviour' was seen by companies as being least material for stakeholder relationships. For company profitability the principles 'Accountability' and 'Transparency' were considered the least material. Moreover, the results of the research indicated that almost 90% of the respondents (among whom were also SME consultants) thought that the principles were too remote from the daily operations of SMEs. In addition, respondents noted that several principles were similar to core subjects.

Figure V.1 **Materiality of the SR principle to SMEs**

Source: IISD 2008

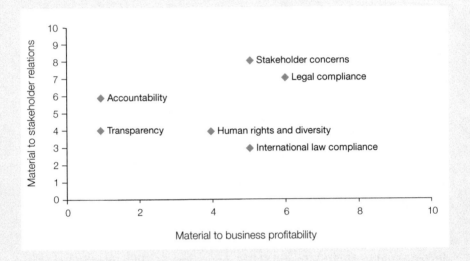

V.3 **How material are the core subjects and issues for SMEs?**

The IISD study also looked at the degree to which the core subjects and issues in ISO 26000 were perceived as being material by SMEs. When this is plotted on the same axes as the principles, a somewhat disappointing result emerges. If the criterion for becoming a material issue is a score of at least six out of ten for both materiality in terms of profitability and materiality in terms of stakeholder relationships, only ten of the ISO 26000 issues are seen as being material by SMEs. According to this analysis, within the core subject 'Human rights', not a single issue is perceived as being material. Examples of ISO 26000 issues that are seen as material by SMEs are 'Health and safety at work' (core subject 'Labour practices'), 'Climate change mitigation and adaptation' (core subject 'The environment') and 'Social investment' (core subject 'Community involvement and development'). The overall picture, however, is that the core subjects and issues are seen as being of limited relevance, and that only a small number of issues score high (nine out of ten or higher) on materiality in terms of profitability or on materiality in terms of stakeholder relationships—not on both aspects.

V.4 **Can ISO 26000 be applied by SMEs at all?**

The IISD study concludes that the aim of ISO 26000 to be applicable for all kinds of organisations, irrespective of the sector in which they operate and their size, is not realistic. The SMEs for which ISO 26000 has some relevance are companies that are export-oriented, part of international supply chains, produce products or services that have a focus on society or the environment, are financed by ethical investors, or are led by people who already value the importance of sustainable development. This is clearly a small percentage of SMEs. Our own research (Brandsma *et al.* 2009) supports the IISD's conclusions. In the category 'organisations with less than 50 employees' a very small percentage of respondents are considering using ISO 26000.

Does this mean that ISO 26000 is of little or even no value at all for SMEs? Despite the above, the IISD (and ourselves) believe that the answer to this question is no. The quoted research focuses on the SR core subjects and issues and their relevance to SMEs. However, this is not the only aspect of SR the guideline advises on. It also helps organisations to realise stakeholder engagement and advises on the process of determining the social responsibility of an organisation. This 'double approach', focusing on subjects, but also on the process of implementation, clears the path for the guideline to become a comprehensive guide for introducing SMEs to SR, and the fact that it allows for flexibility in how it is applied to an organisation-specific interpretation of SR actually enhances its applicability.

SMEs that want to base their SR policies on ISO 26000 should use the flexibility of the guideline to the greatest extent possible and work 'in the spirit of' ISO 26000; they should not be overly focused on the SR core subjects and issues specified in the guideline. Finally, they should follow the suggestions on the *process* for determining the social responsibilities of companies and the implementation of these responsibilities. This is where we feel that the guideline truly adds value and makes for a good point of departure for every organisation wanting to implement SR.

7
Selecting SR priorities

7.1 **Introduction**

SR is often criticised as being an open book—a catch-all heading encompassing a huge number of themes. This can make social responsibility a daunting area to integrate into the strategic life of an organisation. The challenge is to identify the unique and specific impact areas an organisation has, which vary according to the context in which it operates and the characteristics of its operations. But how does an organisation decide which sustainability impacts it has and, subsequently, how these can be managed? Nobody benefits from a broad, uninspiring interpretation of SR—neither the organisation nor society. Selecting SR priorities, based on thorough analyses and organisational ambition is crucial to any SR policy. ISO 26000, as we have already argued, is a useful tool in this respect, as it leaves organisations with enough space to develop such an organisation-specific approach to SR. It sets out SR principles and SR core subjects, but the real added value comes with the acknowledgement that every organisation has a specific SR profile *and*, in offering organisations guidance in order to determine their own profile, an organisational-specific approach.

One of the key requirements in producing a SR profile is acknowledging and measuring the social and ecological footprints—or sustainability impacts—of the organisation. Which SR impact areas affect the organisation? Which ones are the most important? Which activities create the most significant sustainability effects? And to what degree can an organisation influence these? This is, in essence, what the first part of the final of the four central clauses (Clauses 4–7) within ISO 26000 deals with: 'Guidance on integrating social responsibility throughout an organisation'.

This chapter discusses the first part of Clause 7—selecting SR priorities that fit the organisation. The most important concepts related to determining SR priorities are 'relevance', 'significance' and 'sphere of influence'. These are sequentially discussed and illustrated by the most important passages in ISO 26000 concerning these concepts. The chapter ends with useful tools and methods for selecting the SR priorities of the organisation.

7.2 Relevance and significance

ISO 26000—and other SR-related guidelines—use relevance and significance as key criteria for determining the SR priorities of an organisation. For example, in the GRI guidelines for sustainability reporting it is stated that an organisation should determine the report's boundaries by consecutively identifying: what sustainability indicators and SR core subjects and issues are relevant for the organisation; what are the significant consequences for sustainable development; and on which of these subjects and issues can the organisation exercise a certain degree of influence. In ISO 26000 relevance, significance and sphere of influence are also import criteria in determining which issues are important to the organisation (ISO 2010: 71-72).

In order to analyse how organisational activities and characteristics are related to the SR core subjects and issues, an organisation should perform an impact analysis based on relevance, significance and influence. An impact analysis essentially shows an organisation where its ecological and social footprint is, who is affected by it, and what effects it can influence and how. Although an organisation may understand the relevant societal expectations, assessing its activities by relevance, significance and sphere of influence

1 Anders Bekken blog, 'De PricewaterhouseCoopers Duurzaamheidbarometer: Duurzaamheid onderdeel strategie', 13 October 2009; www.stichtingmilieunet.nl/andersbekekenblog/duurzaam/de-pricewaterhousecoopers-duurzaamheidbarometer-duurzaamheid-heeft-een-vaste-positie-veroverd.html, accessed 19 March 2011.

should also involve its (internal and external) stakeholders in assessing the SR core subjects and issues that the organisation has to deal with.

In Chapter 2 we discussed the interpretation of (C)SR, according to ISO 26000 and argued that organisations should understand three types of relationships: the relationship between the organisation and society; the relationship between the organisation and its stakeholders; and the relationship between the organisation's stakeholders and society. Impact—the internal and external effects of the organisation—is a crucial element in these relationships and ISO 26000 states that organisations are accountable for their sustainability impact (also see the principle of accountability as described in Chapter 4).

Organisations, according to the guideline, should understand how their activities, processes, products, services and decisions impact society, stakeholders and the environment. They should also understand what expectations society has regarding these impacts. In addition, the effect of the organisation on and through different stakeholders can be part of its impact analysis.[2]

However, as we have already seen, ISO 26000 makes an important distinction between the relevance and significance of SR impact areas. All SR core subjects (but *not* all SR issues that are specified under these core subjects) are, to a greater or lesser extent, relevant to any organisation. The degree of relevance is left to the organisation to decide for itself. The organisation's most important SR impact areas in terms of sustainability impact (where the organisation has a significant social or ecological footprint) must at least be part of its SR profile. If this were not the case, the organisation's SR policy would lack credibility and likely face failure.

7.2.1 Relevance

Many SR issues could be relevant for an organisation—and not just those identified in ISO 26000. The organisation need not be too selective at this stage. The most important requirement here is to make sure nothing is omitted from what is essentially a long-list. Shortening the list based on significance and ranking the SR impact areas is something for later concern. To develop the list of relevant SR impact areas, the organisation should identify the full range of its activities, its stakeholders, and the organisations that are in

---

2 Or as the SR guideline puts it (ISO 2010: 16): 'When recognising the core subjects and issues of its social responsibility, an organisation is helped by considering interactions with other organisations. An organisation should also consider the impact of its decisions and activities on stakeholders.'

its sphere of influence, including suppliers and subcontractors. It also needs to list all SR issues that are related to its daily operations and activities, both under normal and very specific circumstances. For the full 'to do' list see page 71 of ISO 26000 (2101).

'Under very specific circumstances' refers to unusual activities such as the opening of a new production facility, headquarters or office. In this example, SR impact areas such as energy efficiency (for example, by applying innovative production technologies), CO_2 emissions caused by commuting and work traffic (the location of the new office/public transport links) and disabled access would be very relevant.

Although an organisation may be able to map the relevant SR impact areas and societal expectations concerning its mission, its activities and its social responsibilities, it is highly recommended that both external and internal stakeholders be involved in the process—even if this takes the form of testing the organisation's own results against those of its stakeholders. The chances are that this will result in new insights, perhaps regarding which SR impact areas are and are not covered by laws and regulations in certain countries. Further input could come, for example, from trade or sector organisations, industry bodies or SR knowledge centres, such as CSR Europe. A few examples of common SR impact areas for certain industries are displayed in Box 7.1.

After the 'mapping exercise' has been completed a comprehensive list of SR impact areas can be drawn up. The organisation should still bear in mind that it is unlikely to be *completely* comprehensive. Relevant SR impact areas can change in the (near) future (just as can the relevant stakeholders the organisation engages with). Once the idea of ever-changing impact areas is recognised, the organisation should regularly re-evaluate its priorities and, when and where necessary, adjust, supplement or shorten them in order to keep the list of priorities up to date (ISO 2010: 73)

7.2.2 Significance

Once the organisation has a complete picture of its relevant SR impact areas, the next step is to make a selection to reduce the length of the list to more workable proportions. This should be done by identifying the impact areas that are the most important to the organisation in terms of sustainability. The organisation should methodically map its biggest social and ecological footprints.[3]

---

3 'The significance of an impact should be considered with reference both to the stakeholders concerned and to the way in which the impact affects sustainable development' (ISO 2010: 16).

Box 7.1 **SR impact areas in several industries**

Even though SR impact areas may only be partly comparable for organisations in different sectors, there are commonalities between certain
sector-specific SR issues and topics. We look at three sectors below
and mention a few sector-specific SR issues that their respective Dutch
trade organisations have identified together with CSR Netherlands as
important:

Caterers

- Sustainable purchasing: providing fair trade, organic, local and sea-
  sonal products
- Health: providing healthy products and lifestyle promotion
- Packaging: reducing individual packages for every serving and using
  recyclable packaging material
- Energy: improving energy efficiency and reducing CO emissions
- Waste: reducing food waste

Technical services providers

- Sustainable products: selling and installing energy- and water-effi-
  cient products and installations
- Sustainable material use: efficiently dealing with the use and disposal of materials, and purchasing sustainable materials
- Recruitment of employees: offering good working conditions and
  internships
- Integral design: delivering economically, ecologically, aesthetically
  and socially useful design from architect to plumber
- Societal engagement: providing time, money and/or means for the
  benefit of the local community

Removal contractors

- Emissions of greenhouse gases: reducing the use of fossil fuels in
  trucks
- Climate compensation: compensating CO_2 emissions
- Safety and (physical) health: ensuring safe and healthy working
  conditions
- Traffic safety: encouraging responsible driving leading to fewer accidents and less fuel consumption
- Transparency: offering insights into the environmental and social
  effects of services and activities

Eventually, these SR impact areas will make up the core of the SR profile of the organisation which it will use to determine content of its SR policy. In order to decide on the importance of an impact, an organisation should develop selection criteria. ISO 26000 provides several suggestions for possible criteria, such as the amount of impact of the respective core subjects on society and the organisation's stakeholders, the organisation's SR performance *vis-à-vis* international standards and best practice, and the extent to which stakeholders are concerned about a SR issue. Furthermore, one can also think of the potential effect of (not) taking action on an issue or the relation between the necessary resources to take a certain action versus the potential (positive or negative) effects (ISO 2010: 72). Many organisations will welcome the fact that ISO 26000 recognises proportionality. In other words, the importance of an impact area must justify the efforts an organisation puts into managing it.

Another term for a significant impact area is a 'material impact area'. Materiality is a term often used in accountancy to indicate which topics and information are necessary in order to make the right decisions, or where the omission of that information influences the financial decisions that are based on it. Material information should therefore always be included in annual reports. This term is also used in the GRI guidelines for sustainability reporting to indicate important impact areas (in line with the approach of ISO 26000). Organisations can perform a materiality test (see Box 7.2) as part of the process of determining their societal responsibilities. Stakeholder dialogue is important here—just as it is with mapping relevant impact areas, and ISO 26000 encourages increased stakeholder engagement. However, the mission and ambition of an organisation evidently also play an important role in determining the important material impact areas and if stakeholder consultation does not underline the importance of a known issue, the organisation must declare its relevance.[4]

4 'Although an organisation itself may believe it understands its social responsibility [. . .], it should nevertheless consider involving stakeholders in the identification process to broaden the perspective on the core subjects and issues. It is important to recognise, though, that issues may be relevant even if stakeholders fail to identify them' (ISO 2010: 71).

Box 7.2 **Determining materiality according to GRI**

Source: *Sustainability Reporting Guidelines: Version 3* (GRI 2006: 9)

The information in a sustainability report should cover topics and indicators that reflect the most important economic, environmental and social effects that can substantially influence the decisions of stakeholders. A combination of internal and external factors should be used to determine whether the information is material or not.

External factors

When defining material subjects external factors need to be taken into account, among others:

- The most important sustainability interests/subjects/indicators that stakeholders come up with
- The most important subjects are future challenges for the sector about which colleagues and competitors report
- Relevant laws, rules, international agreements or voluntary agreements that are of strategic importance for the organisation and its stakeholders
- Reasonable estimation of sustainability effects, risks or chances (for example, climate change, HIV/AIDS, poverty) that are mapped by means of robust research by people with an acknowledged expertise or by acknowledged professional bodies with credentials in the field.

Internal factors

When defining material subjects, internal factors have to be taken into account, among others:

- Important organisation values, policies, strategies, operational management systems, aims and goals set
- The interests/expectations of stakeholders that have a specific interest in the organisation (for example, employees, shareholders and suppliers)
- Significant risks for the organisation
- Critical factors for enabling organisational success
- The core competencies of the organisation and the way in which these (could) contribute to sustainable development

7.3 **Sphere of influence**

In the previous sections the terms 'influence' and 'sphere of influence' have already been briefly discussed, but not elaborated on.[5] This is an important area, as organisations are very likely to have a significant sustainability impact in their sphere of influence and have scope to make a difference. When an organisation considers its long-list of SR impact areas, there are likely to be a number of topics in which the influence it can exert is minimal or non-existent. For example, it may be a minor partner in a project, or be dependent on or limited by legislation.

When dealing with SR-related issues, situations can emerge in which the ability of an organisation to influence others will also coincide with its responsibility to exercise this influence.[6] The ability of the organisation to influence others can be derived from several sources. It can originate from the fact that the organisation is a large player in the market and therefore purchases large quantities of products or services, so one can speak of its economic purchasing power. A good example here is the sustainable purchasing initiative by the Dutch government. The Dutch government buys approximately €40 billion of goods and services every year. This gives it considerable influence and, therefore, responsibility in the customer–supplier relationship. It can be a force for good through its sphere of influence. Another kind of economic dependency arises when an organisation is a player with a certain, unique characteristic. An example

---

5 ISO 26000 defines an organisation's sphere of influence as (ISO 2010: 4): 'Range/ extent of political, contractual, economic or other relationships through which an organisation [. . .] has the ability to affect the decisions or activities of individuals or organisations.'

6 On this matter ISO 26000 states (ISO 2010: 72): 'An organisation can exercise its influence with others either to enhance positive impacts on sustainable development, or to minimise negative impacts, or both. When assessing its sphere of influence and determining its responsibilities, an organisation should exercise due diligence.'

7 Business in the Community, *Survey Report of Consumer Attitudes in Ireland towards Corporate Responsibility* (Dublin: Business in the Community Ireland, 2009): 6.

of this is a highly specialised company that has one or more suppliers that are specialised to such a degree that they cannot sell their product or service to any other party. Influence can also originate elsewhere, such as through a long and intensive cooperation or a shared vision or ambition between several organisations. In the same way, leadership can be an effective source of influence. An organisation can also derive influence from the ownership of shares in another organisation or through its legal mandate.

7.3.1 Determining influence in all SR areas

Now, the question arises: on which of the important impact areas that the organisation has identified does it have an influence, and how great is that influence? ISO 26000 refers to 'sufficient' influence and states that the organisation should practice due diligence when determining this and should consider engaging with stakeholders (ISO 2010: 70). Ideally, the organisation has sufficient influence on its most important SR impact areas, so that by taking action, it can have a real impact. Of course, 'sufficient influence' is open to interpretation—what one person thinks of as sufficient, another will perceive as being too little and yet another as being more than sufficient. Therefore, it is essential to determine whether, when looking at the SR impact areas (and the goals the organisation has formulated regarding those) the current level of influence the organisation has is enough or should it be increased to realise the desired outcomes. When the organisation reaches the conclusion that a specific SR impact area does not lie within its sphere of influence, but considers that this would nevertheless be desirable, the organisation should ask itself whether it has the capability to still realise the desired outcomes. Credibility, again, is the key word here: if a particular SR impact area is of crucial importance for the SR profile of the organisation because the organisation has or can have a large sustainability impact, it might be wise to free up and invest additional resources.

Of course, the ideal picture is often not even close to reality—on the contrary. Therefore, it is very useful to find out which important SR impact areas the organisation can or cannot influence. This way an organisation can proactively engage with its stakeholders in pursuit of why it does not address all its important impact areas and simultaneously demonstrate the ways it does its utmost to broaden its sphere of influence. In this context, ISO 26000 states that an organisation cannot be held responsible for every impact of all parties or factors on which it can exert any form of influence (ISO 2010: 16). However, as has become clear already, there can be situations in which the ability of an organisation to influence others is accompanied by a responsibility to actually exert that influence. An example might be the moral duty to denounce human rights violations by third parties. In general it is argued that the responsibility to exert influence grows when the ability to influence grows. Here the water gets muddy. For example, if organisation A has a relationship with organisation B, it could be argued that A has a responsibility to limit or avoid the negative effects caused by B. Thus, the impact of organisation A does not stop at its boundaries.[8]

The impact/influence matrix in Figure 7.1 offers a method to come to an overview of the SR impact areas, divided into the influence and impact that the organisation has on them. Moreover, the matrix is a first step towards an action plan in which the necessary actions are identified in order to bring impact areas within the desired sphere of influence of the organisation. The matrix can be used as an instrument to differentiate between 'relevant SR impact areas' and 'significant SR impact areas'.

Figure 7.1 **Impact/influence matrix**

	Little impact	**Large impact**
Little influence	Quadrant 1	Quadrant 3
Large influence	Quadrant 2	Quadrant 4

In quadrant 1, SR impact areas should be included where the organisation has little sustainability impact and on which it has little influence. These SR impact areas do not deserve priority in the organisation and addressing with them bestows no benefit on either the organisation or society. The SR impact areas in quadrant 2 are characterised by the fact that the organisation has little sustainability impact, but does have a lot of influence on them. Since the organisation has a lot of influence, it can choose to make an effort in these areas, despite the fact that they have little impact. For example, it could be that the organisation aims to operate in a completely climate-neutral way or as energy-efficiently as possible, and does not want to leave any stone unturned in reaching those goals. There may also be the possibility to realise some form of added value, such as diminishing costs, strengthening the organisation's reputation or because there is a specific stakeholder who would appreciate action. When none of these factors applies, the advice would be similar to that in quadrant 1—there is little to gain for either the organisation or society in addressing these impact areas. In quadrant 3 the organisation

8 'An organisation is responsible for the impacts of decisions and activities over which it has formal and/or de facto control. Such impacts can be extensive' (ISO 2010: 16).

should include SR impact areas where it has significant sustainability impacts but where its influence is limited. These are the most difficult impact areas to address. The dilemma for the organisation is whether to increase its influence on these impact areas or ignore them. This is actually a rhetorical question, since the SR profile of any organisation can only be taken seriously when the organisation pays attention specifically to the impact areas where impact is greatest. After all, this is where the core of its social and ecological footprint is found. The strategy in this quadrant should therefore ideally be to increase the organisation's influence. This, of course, may be difficult. The organisation may be too small to influence others in its sector or the financial investment required may to too great.[9] When this situation arises, the organisation should frankly and proactively explain why it cannot take action. In quadrant 4 the organisation should include those SR impact areas where it has significant sustainability impacts that lie in its direct sphere of influence. These are the impact areas where action truly matters. There is only one suitable strategy here: to make these impact areas part of the SR policy of the organisation and act on them.

A number of issues should be clarified here. First, it is neither necessary nor feasible that an organisation immediately embraces and rolls out strategies for all of its SR impact areas at the same time. For example, an organisation could follow a growth or cascade model for the different SR impact areas. ISO 26000 certainly does not

Did you know...

In the second quarter of 2009 globally 25% more patents for 'clean' technologies were being granted than in the same quarter in 2008.[10]

set a fixed order for dealing with them. This way, an organisation can decide to first direct its attention to the so-called 'low-hanging fruit' and get some quick results. This can be a motivating factor and a stepping stone towards other, more difficult, SR impact areas. However, while not prescribing which impact areas an organisation should deal with first, ISO 26000 does stress that it is necessary to determine long-term goals; so, in tandem with quick results, an organisation should also present a strategic vision on how it might deal with

---

9 An organisation can also decide that the necessary investments are not in proportion to the sustainability impact that can be realised, despite the fact that it is one of the most important SR impact areas. Here, it can be said that something is lacking with regard to the level of the organisation's SR ambitions.

10 'Heslin Rothenberg Farley & Mesiti P.C. announces clean energy patent growth index results through 2nd quarter 2009: CEPGI hits record high', press release, 20 August 2009; www.hrfmlaw.com/img/articles/article_575647.pdf, accessed 19 March 2011.

more intractable and time-consuming goals where, for example, it may need to increase its sphere of influence.[11]

Second, other factors might be important to consider when deciding whether to include one or more SR impact areas in the SR profile of an organisation. For example, the visibility of the SR impact area and the current efforts of the organisation on it. A pragmatic approach can he helpful here. If a particular impact area only has a small sustainability impact, but the organisation can clearly benefit from actions related to this impact area, for instance because they are visible to customers, then it can decide to invest in them. The same kind of consideration can be made by an organisation when a certain stakeholder places a lot of value on the fact that the organisation makes a contribution to, or an investment in, a certain SR impact area. The mission of the organisation (or a particular interest or concern of the CEO/director/owner, for example) could also be a legitimate consideration. In any case, it is up to the organisation to judge these considerations wisely and make sure that in determining the important impact areas it wants to focus on, it is not led *only* by this kind of consideration.

Third, it should be noted that an organisation should also map the sustainability impacts of organisations with which it cooperates in order to get a complete overview of its own sustainability impact. The reach and, therefore, impact of an organisation goes well beyond its own boundaries.

7.3.2 Exercising influence

ISO 26000 specifies different instruments for organisations to exercise influence, both directly and as strategies to bring SR impact areas within the sphere of influence of the organisation. These methods of exercising influence include (ISO 2010: 72-73) are:

- Setting contractual provisions or incentives

- Public statements by the organization

- Engaging with the community, political leaders and other stakeholders

---

11 ISO 260000 acknowledges this (ISO 2010: 75): 'It is also important to recognise that the process of integrating social responsibility throughout an organisation does not occur all at once or at the same pace for all core subjects and issues. It may be helpful to develop a plan for addressing some social responsibility issues in the short term and some over a longer period of time. Such a plan should be realistic and should take into account the capabilities of the organisation, the resources available and the priority of the issues.'

- Making investment decisions

- Sharing knowledge and information

- Conducting joint projects

- Undertaking responsible lobbying and using media relations

- Promoting good practices

- Forming partnerships with sector associations, organisations and others

The daily decisions an organisation makes that affect others, such as subcontractors or business partners, are also clearly important here.[12]

The guideline emphasises that organisations should exercise influence in an ethical way and that dialogue is preferred over other, more power-oriented strategies. Organisations are also advised to, where applicable (for instance, in developing countries), involve governments and government institutions when they exercise influence. Finally, it can be concluded that, according to ISO 26000, when organisations have influence, they also have a responsibility to exercise this influence. This relates to the 'iron law of social responsibility', proposed by Keith Davis in 1973. This law states that, in the long run, those who do not use their power in a way that society deems responsible, will probably lose power. Davis observes, 'social responsibilities of businessmen need to be commensurate with their social power' (cited by Carroll 1999: 271).

7.4 **Setting SR priorities**

The foundations for selecting SR priorities come from the mapping of relevant impact areas, identifying which of these is significant and determining the sphere of influence the organisation has in each. Here, ISO 26000 provides organisations with the freedom for an organisation-specific interpretation of SR. Every organisation, after all, has its own, unique social and ecological footprint. Moreover, ISO 26000 is not overly prescriptive in the sense that

---

12 For example, ISO 26000 states (ISO 2010: 73): 'An organisation should consider the environmental, social and organisational governance aspects and the social responsibility of the organisations with which it has or seeks to have a relationship. An organisation can influence its stakeholders through its decisions and activities, and through the information that it provides to stakeholders about the basis for these decisions and activities.'

it does not require an organisation to deal with its sustainability impact at all cost: rather, investments should be balanced with aspirations and the resources an organisation has. Credibility is required, though. An organisation cannot ignore areas where it has a great sustainability impact. This is where its efforts should be focused.

When selecting SR priorities an organisation should, according to ISO 26000, give high priority to SR impact areas and activities that have important implications for sustainable development. Also, an organisation can give high priority to SR impact areas and activities that might have a considerable effect on the social responsibilities of the organisation. These constitute different categories. The first category specifically refers to SR impact areas and actions that are related to, among other things, legal compliance and which are consistent with international norms of behaviour and practices and activities that have severe environmental and social effects. High priority based on significance for sustainable development should be given to issues and actions that relate to (ISO 2010: 70):

- Compliance with the law and international norms of behaviour

- Potential violations of human rights

- Practices that could endanger life or health

- Practices that could seriously affect the environment

- Issues where the organization's performance is well below best practice

Regarding the second category, ISO 26000 refers to actions that have a high priority based on the effect the issues or actions could have on the organisation's social responsibility. These could be assigned to actions that (ISO 2010: 70):

- Will take a long time to become fully effective

- Are of immediate concern to stakeholders

---

13 Centraal Bureau voor de Statistiek, *Monitor Duurzaam Nederland 2009* (Den Haag: Centraal Bureau voor de Statistiek, 2009): 206

- May significantly improve the ability of the organisation to meet important objectives

- Have significant cost implications if not addressed quickly

- Can be implemented quickly and easily and will therefore be useful in increasing awareness of and motivation for action on social responsibility within the organisation

Not every organisation will have the same list of priorities, and the ranking order of priorities will differ between organisations.[14] Moreover, the SR priorities of an organisation should be periodically revised and updated. Obviously, organisations can use the material and significant issues that stakeholders expect as identified in ISO 26000 as their priorities, but every organisation is free to phrase or rephrase the issues in order for them to fit with the organisational language and culture (see Box 7.3).

7.5 **Final comments**

This chapter has dealt with how ISO 26000 proposes integrating SR into organisations' daily activities, processes, products, services and decision-making. The way in which an organisation lives up to its social responsibilities should be dependent on its specific characteristics and context. That is why the distinction that ISO 26000 makes between relevant and significant SR impact areas is very important: an organisation should focus on its own material impact areas. That is sensible not only from the perspective of credibility (since this is where the organisation has its significant sustainability footprint), but also from an economic perspective (an organisation does not have unlimited resources to respectively minimise and maximise all of its negative and positive effects). Furthermore, it is important that an organisation does everything possible to make use of its influence in order to promote SR in its supply chain and with partners.

The next chapter will discuss the second part of Clause 7 and deal with the relevant aspects of SR implementation.

---

14 In addition to setting priorities for direct action, ISO 26000 states that (ISO 2010: 73): '[A]n organisation can establish priorities for consideration of issues that are relevant to decisions and activities that an organisation expects to carry out in the future, such as building construction, employing new staff, hiring contractors or conducting fund-raising activities. The priority considerations will then form part of the planning for these future activities.'

Box 7.3 **Examples of CSR priorities**

Almost every organisation phrases its CSR priorities in such a way to match the organisational language or culture, but also to make sure it matches with the expectations of stakeholders. Below are three examples:

Air France KLM: 'The 5 Group CSR policy priorities'

- To combat climate change
- To reduce our environmental footprint
- To build sustainable relations with our customers
- To promote a responsible HR policy
- To contribute to local and global development[a]

University of Plymouth, UK: 'The 4C approach'

- Curriculum: the University commits to engaging students at all levels with sustainability concepts and issues
- Campus: the University commits to campus (building, landscaping, procurement, catering, transport and social) practices that contribute to the achievement of cultural, economic, environmental and social sustainability
- Community: the University acknowledges that it has a leading role to play in advancing the sustainability agenda in the South West of England and will continue to develop regional partnerships and networks in this regard
- Culture: to achieve its sustainability goals, the University recognises that it must develop as an adaptive learning (not just teaching) organisation, a process in which both staff and students have key roles to play[b]

John Keells Group: 'CSR focus areas'

The John Keells Group is the largest listed conglomerate on the Sri Lanka stock exchange and is active in several industries such as transportation, leisure, property, financial services, consumer food and retail and information technology. The Group has identified the following CSR focus areas:

a AFI KLM E&M, 'The 5 Group CSR Policy Priorities'; www.afiklmem.com/ AFIKLMEM/en/g_page_standard/SustainableDevelopment/5Priorities.html, accessed 21 March 2011.

b 'University of Plymouth Sustainability Policy: Summary'; csf.plymouth.ac.uk/files/ UPSUSTPOLICY12.pdf, accessed 21 March 2011.

- Education: The John Keells Group believes that education is the foundation stone of an enlightened and civilised society
- Health: The John Keells Group believes that a healthy society is a productive one
- Community/Livelihood Development: The John Keells Group reaches out to the communities surrounding its operations through constructive dialogue with stakeholders and staff volunteerism, translating into a range of community service initiatives
- Environment: the Sustainability Initiative of the John Keells Group drives efforts at minimising the impact of the Group's operations on the environment to conserve and promote the environment for the well-being of present and future generations
- Arts and Culture: The John Keells Group is committed to sponsoring arts and culture towards safeguarding and promoting the cultural heritage of the community
- Disaster relief
- Sustainable sourcing: John Keells has recognised that developing a sustainable sourcing mechanism in a company's supply chain can raise productivity, enhance customer–supplier relations, support innovation, and enable growth[c]

c John Keells Group, 'More than 140 Years of Corporate Citizenship'; www.keells. com/csr-home.html, accessed 21 March 2011.

8

SR implementation

8.1 **Introduction**

In Chapter 7 we discussed the first part of Clause 7 of ISO 26000. Chapter 8 is entirely devoted to the second part of this clause: the implementation of SR—putting into practice the societal responsibilities of an organisation. SR should be an integral part of both long-term decision-making and the day-to-day activities of organisations; from strategy to operations.[1]

This is a critical area because the successful implementation of SR is clearly a big challenge for many organisations. There are a number of difficulties and barriers that organisations can experience in practice, including creating enthusiasm and fostering engagement with SR. ISO 26000 gives special attention to communicating SR in organisations, increasing the credibility of SR initiatives and improving SR performance. These topics are dealt with in this chapter.

But this chapter's main aim is to give an overview of how ISO 26000 recommends organisations to proceed with the implementation of SR, what

---

1 'Because social responsibility concerns the potential and actual impacts of an organisation's decisions and activities, the ongoing, regular daily activities of the organisation constitute the most important behaviour to be addressed. Social responsibility should be an integral part of core organisational strategy with assigned responsibilities and accountability at all appropriate levels of the organisation. It should be reflected in decision-making and considered in implementing activities' (ISO 2010: 7).

kind of actions they should take to successfully do this, and how they should subsequently monitor and improve SR activities and performance.

8.2 **This is not starting from scratch**

Just as it is a misunderstanding to assume that SR is a fairly new phenomenon, it is also wrong to believe that SR is entirely new for organisations. We would argue that every organisation already undertakes certain SR activities in a way that goes beyond compliance with the law. It is self-evident, however, that large differences in the degree of engagement with SR exists between organisations.[2]

Therefore, in general, organisations do not have to start from scratch when putting SR into practice. This same realistic point of departure is used within ISO 26000—connecting existing systems and structures will be a wise and feasible option for many organisations.[3]

This idea fits with the overall aim of ISO 26000: to become an all-encompassing guideline that does not want to replace other initiatives, but instead, to offer a SR framework to organise current and future initiatives. This is a realistic and sensible point of departure for SR implementation, since it acknowledges initiatives already being undertaken by organisations and offers a head start for the process. For example, many organisations are already dealing with core subjects such as 'Labour practices' or 'Consumer issues'. For leaders in the SR field, it may be argued that ISO 26000 is less useful. They may already have a SR strategy embedded, be using the guidelines of the GRI to communicate their efforts, and/or be developing new and responsible products and services. They may not see the sense in reinventing the wheel. However, in

2 It is also a misconception to believe that very many organisations are already practising SR perfectly. Many certainly claim or believe this to be the case but, in truth, few are. Without wishing to belittle the work of the true leaders who have SR strategies deeply embedded in the fabric of their organisations, we believe that one should be cautious about the myriad claims—from new start-ups to Fortune 500 organisations. Besides, in this book, it has been argued several times already that SR is a process of continuous improvement and therefore never truly finished—a notion that is supported by ISO 26000.

3 'In most cases, organisations can build on existing systems, policies, structures and networks of the organisation to put social responsibility into practice, although some activities are likely to be conducted in new ways, or with consideration for a broader range of factors' (ISO 2010: 67).

principle, ISO 26000 is meant for all types of organisations, irrespective of their point of departure.

8.2.1 Barriers to SR implementation

ISO 26000 stresses that connecting SR to the culture, values and thus the identity of the organisation will have a positive effect on understanding and acceptance which, in turn, can facilitate and speed up the implementation process. Resistance to change is a likely obstacle and organisational culture cannot be changed overnight, but connecting SR to the culture of the organisation seems a sensible approach. Organisations where the culture and values are already aligned with SR and its principles will, of course, experience less difficulties with its further development.[5]

Did you know...

The Pricewaterhouse-Coopers' Sustainability barometer of September 2009 showed that 70% of Dutch companies of all sizes do not have plans to change their current initiatives and investments in the field of sustainability as a consequence of the economic crisis. The most important reason for this is the fact that sustainability forms an integral part of their business.[4]

Organisational change tends to be a long-term process—taking not weeks or months, but likely years to be realised. Nor is it smooth or problem-free either, but likely a bumpy and messy process. An evolutionary journey, in fact. Therefore, perseverance is often necessary. Moreover, the implementation of different SR core subjects and issues in different parts of an organisation does not take the same amount of time. Our own research (with Dutch companies) showed that around 68% of the organisations we talked to about the implementation of their SR policy were happy with their progress (Brandsma *et al.* 2009). Organisations were also asked to indicate the most important barriers to SR implementation. The most important was the lack of an overarching framework: an obstacle that might be eliminated by ISO 26000. Other key obstacles included obtaining buy-in from the board and the economic situation (see Table 8.1).

---

4 Anders Bekken blog, 'De PricewaterhouseCoopers Duurzaamheidbarometer: Duurzaamheid onderdeel strategie', 13 October 2009; www.stichtingmilieunet.nl/andersbekekenblog/duurzaam/ de-pricewaterhousecoopers-duurzaamheidbarometer-duurzaamheid-heeft-een-vaste-positie-veroverd.html, accessed 19 March 2011.

5 'Creating a culture of social responsibility within an organisation may take a substantial period of time, but proceeding systematically and working from existing values and cultures have been effective in many organisations' (ISO 2010: 74).

Table 8.1 **Barriers to SR implementation**

Source: Brandsma *et al.* 2009

Barrier	% of organisations citing barrier
Lack of a clear action plan	56.8%
Too little time available	47.7%
Too little knowledge about SR implementation	43.2%
Too little knowledge of SR	38.6%
Obtaining buy-in from the board	31.8%
The economic crisis	25.0%
Too little budget available	20.5%
Creating engagement with employees	15.9%
Creating engagement with middle management	13.6%

As discussed in the previous chapter, it is possible and recommendable to try and achieve short-term successes to kick-start SR implementation. Such quick wins or low-hanging fruit can increase enthusiasm for SR initiatives as well as making SR more visible throughout the organisation. Tangible results are produced and the SR efforts and investments made in the past are acknowledged. Community involvement is an area many organisations have a track record in and, as a key element of ISO 26000, and because such initiatives often have tangible and visible effects and already have employee support, it can act as a lightning conductor for SR efforts.

With the development of an organisation-specific SR profile that fits the culture and mission of an organisation, many of the barriers identified by our research can be overcome. Buy-in from the leadership should already be assured and policies for proper engagement and generating enthusiasm for SR, connecting with existing systems such as quality or health and safety, and organising new processes and activities will progress better. The development of a SR profile is essentially the first step towards implementing SR. This idea of SR fitting with the culture of the organisation is extremely important in terms of communicating initiatives. Each organisation has its own language—'the way things are done here'. A SR programme should be communicated no differently. This may be formal or informal. In the former, the organisation might talk of a 'SR business plan', while a target-oriented organisational culture could consider setting targets for its SR work.[6]

6 See also Chapter 3 of this book.

8.3 **Support for SR from the top—but not only from the top**

The strategic level of an organisation is where the direction and aims of the organisation are decided upon—this should also be the case for SR. A commitment from the top of an organisation is an important prerequisite to making any initiative work. This is where putting SR into practice starts to succeed—or fail. The board of directors may, for instance, pay lip-service to SR initiatives. This will almost certainly lead to failure. The goals, ambitions, values and ethics of an organisation should be lived and breathed by its top management. Without this, there is no credibility to SR and no real hope that others in the organisation will believe the topic is important.

According to ISO 26000, an organisation should make SR an integral part of its strategy, policies, culture, structure and operations. Some useful actions to integrate SR may include (ISO 2010: 74-75):

- Including in the organisation's aspirations or vision statement reference to the way in which it intends social responsibility to influence its activities

- Incorporating in its purpose or in a mission statement specific, clear and concise references to important aspects of social responsibility, including the principles and issues of social responsibility that help determine the way the organisation operates

- Adopting written codes of conduct or ethics that specify the organisation's commitment to social responsibility by translating the principles and values into statements on appropriate behaviour. Such codes should be based on the principles of social responsibility in Clause 4 and on guidance in Clause 6

- Including social responsibility as a key element of the organisation's strategy, through its integration into systems, policies, processes and decision-making behaviour

- Translating the priorities for action on core subjects and issues into manageable organisational objectives with strategies, processes and timelines. Objectives should be specific and measurable or verifiable. Stakeholder input can be valuable in assisting this process. Detailed plans for achieving the objectives, including responsibilities, timelines, budgets and the effect on other activities of the organisation, should be an important element in establishing the objectives and the strategies for their achievement.

Box 8.1 The CSR vision

Source: www.demeeuw.com

A company is as good as the products that it provides the market with and the means by which it does this. De Meeuw has taken tangible steps to contribute to a healthy, social and prosperous society for years.

Vision

De Meeuw considers cooperation with society and societal well-being as being essential to the long-term 'licence to operate'. Therefore, it wants to be part of a responsible society. By putting corporate social responsibility (CSR) into practice De Meeuw develops values for a healthier, safer and more comfortable living and work environment, and also increases its competitiveness.

Objective

For some time now, initiatives and measures that are related to CSR are gradually getting more embedded and interconnected. The objective therefore is an optimisation of the balance between ecological, societal and economic aspects that the organisation can influence.

Level of ambition

The management team has decided on a gradual increase in the level of CSR within the organisation. This is guided by the motto: 'every step towards a sustainable future is a step forward'. Do what is possible and carry it out with conviction. For some time now for every decision the effect on the environment and society is assessed. Where a negative impact is expected, measures are taken.

It is also important that we, with our way of operating and within our possibilities, want to contribute to sustainability in your organisation. We mainly realise this by a particularly low percentage of project failure and by linking minimal road transportation to the stock capacity and functionality of your housing. By doing this, we create buildings that have long life-spans, retain the best employees, manage our waste responsibly and limit our CO_2 emissions.

Most of these suggestions are relevant for all organisations, irrespective of their characteristics; but, of course, different organisations will have a variety of concerns depending on the context in which they exist.

Box 8.1 gives an example of Dutch construction company De Meeuw's CSR vision.

Developing SR awareness within an organisation and thus among employees plays an important role when integrating SR throughout the entire organisation. Organisations that are at the start of the SR implementation process ought to be aware of the fact that in this phase the emphasis should be on increasing the understanding and awareness of SR and of the relevant aspects and dilemmas for the organisation and the sector in which it operates. When the board of an organisation is aware of the (economic) advantages of SR in the context of sustainable development, or in reaching certain ambitions of the organisation, the chances for a long-term and enduring commitment increase.

8.3.1 Engaging all levels of the organisation

ISO 26000 emphasises that commitment and understanding of SR are necessary at all levels of an organisation. It is likely that employees will have a large diversity of opinions and viewpoints on SR-related issues. Some will have no interest. For others certain issues may be motivating factors to arrive early for work every day. It is towards this second group that organisations may want to target first initiatives. The organisation may, for example, consider empowering and supporting such employees to take ownership of SR initiatives by appointing SR 'ambassadors' or 'champions', or by establishing a 'green team'. In this way, SR projects can stem from or be influenced by the values and beliefs of the employees. There is likely to be enthusiasm, energy and a willingness to make initiatives work, enthuse others and create unexpected wins for the organisation. For example, empowered employees may have suggestions about improving energy efficiency, processes or even innovations to products and services. They may also be useful in developing an organisation's ability to engage with other stakeholders. Such employees should be supported with access to education, training and skills development wherever possible.[7]

---

7 'Education and lifelong learning are central to raising awareness and building competency for social responsibility. In this regard, education for sustainable development is setting a new direction to empower people to address social responsibility issues by encouraging them to have due regard for values that foster vigorous and proactive action' (ISO 2010: 74).

Box 8.2 outlines a number of key success factors for SR implementation. These insights come from research conducted by a Dutch government agency for road and waterways management on international SR champions (Cochius and Moratis 2009).

Box 8.2 **Lessons from leaders**
Source: Cochius and Moratis 2009

In 2008 and 2009 the Dutch government agency for road and waterways management conducted research into successful SR implementation in nine Dutch organisations and a German, a Swedish, a Finnish and a New Zealand organisation from the public and private sectors, known internationally as SR best-practice practitioners. One of the key findings was that these organisations think in terms of 'and–and' instead of 'or–or'. They have achieved success with SR by giving attention to:

- **Both the soft and the hard side:** SR can be found in culture, behaviour, enthusiasm and awareness as well as in strategy, KPIs, department plans, and planning and control cycles
- **Both knowing what and how:** in order to see the relevance of SR, employees have to know what SR means (the bigger picture) and how to put it into practice (daily activities)
- **Both top-down and bottom-up:** at the top of an organisation there has to be a visible commitment to SR, while at the same time employees have to be enthusiastic to start working with it
- **Both isolating and connecting:** the establishment of specific SR activities and projects is essential, as is embedding these activities in the day-to-day processes of the organisation

8.4 **Communicating about SR**

Today, the media is full of communications about SR and sustainability related-issues—cars, healthcare, cleaning products, groceries, etc. We are bombarded with messages about how the good, fair, clean or green products and services we buy are good for us, for our society and the planet. Of course, SR communications can be for a variety of audiences. An organisation would not, for example, necessarily communicate in the same way to a trade union as it would to a potential employee.

In addition, organisations are now required to communicate more to particular audiences on a variety of SR-related issues. Details on purchasing and tendering processes are demanded by clients, shareholders want information on topics such as carbon management strategies, NGOs want to know why an organisation has production facilities in countries where there is conflict or human rights abuses. Organisations are being asked difficult questions and need to provide answers.

ISO 26000 devotes a lot of attention to the communication of SR. Communication is critical to many different functions in social responsibility including (ISO 2010: 76):

Did you know...

Research shows that there is a positive relationship between perceived environmental performance and employee satisfaction.[8]

- Raising awareness both within and outside the organisation on its strategies and objectives, plans, performance and challenges for social responsibility

- Demonstrating respect for the social responsibility principles in Clause 4

- Helping to engage and create dialogue with stakeholders

- Addressing legal and other requirements for the disclosure of information related to social responsibility

- Showing how the organisation is meeting its commitments on social responsibility and responding to the interests of stakeholders and expectations of society in general

- Providing information about the impacts of the organisation's activities, products and services, including details of how the impacts change over time

- Helping to engage and motivate employees and others to support the organisation's activities in social responsibility

- Facilitating comparison with peer organisations, which can stimulate improvements in performance on social responsibility

8 Courtney Rubin, 'Why it's better to be green than to be profitable', *Inc.*, 9 February 2011; www.inc.com/news/articles/2011/02/go-green-for-happy-employees.html, accessed 21 March 2011.

- Enhancing an organisation's reputation for socially responsible action, openness, integrity and accountability, to strengthen stakeholder trust in the organisation

For every communication goal there are suitable channels and instruments available. More attention will be given to this in the coming sections.

8.4.1 Methods of communication

One can think of many different ways to communicate about SR. The available instruments are, in fact, no different than those used to communicate other subjects, but every instrument has its own goals and is suitable for a specific target group. One evident medium is the sustainability or responsibility report (whether or not guided by the GRI guidelines for sustainability reporting), though that mainly remains the domain of large, multinational companies.

Nevertheless, more and more SMEs, such as Gulpener (The Netherlands), VicSuper (Australia), Risk and Policy Analysts (UK), Best Foot Forward (UK), BoxMarche (Italy) and Ecologic Designs (US), release an annual sustainability or social report. Globally, in 2006 around 50 to 60 government organisations also released such a report. However, there are countless other ways to bring the SR commitments and achievements of an organisation to the attention of a wider public or relevant stakeholders. ISO 26000 provides some examples, such as stakeholder meetings, product communications, advertisements and SR-oriented team activities. A range of communication instruments might be used to get a consistent message out to a spectrum of different stakeholders.

Did you know...

In the Netherlands, as opposed to a number of other European countries such as the UK, France or Denmark, there is no law making SR reporting obligatory. However, there is a guide for societal reporting published by the Council for Annual Reporting.[9,10]

ISO 26000 does set out some requirements for SR-related communications. These largely overlap with those in the GRI guidelines. Communication about SR, according to ISO 26000, should be

9 Tom Young, 'Denmark latest to pass CSR reporting law', *BusinessGreen*, 8 January 2009; www.businessgreen.com/bg/news/1801774/denmark-pass-csr-reporting-law, accessed 21 March 2011.

10 Raad voor de Jaarverslaggeving, 'Handreiking voor Maatschappelijke verslaggeving'; www.rjnet.nl/RJ/Richtlijnen/Handreiking+MVO/default.aspx, accessed 21 March 2011.

complete, understandable, responsive to stakeholder interests, accurate, balanced, timely and accessible (ISO 2010: 76). An organisation should hence address all activities and impacts that are significant from a SR perspective and make this information available to all of its stakeholders.

8.4.2 Stakeholder dialogue

ISO 26000 gives considerable attention to the importance of stakeholder dialogue when it comes to SR communication.[11] The most important advantage of a stakeholder dialogue is that an organisation is constantly well informed about the (changing) interests and expectations of its stakeholders. According to ISO 26000, an organisation should search for dialogue with stakeholders in order to: determine whether previous communication efforts were successful, identify priorities for future communications, and develop best practice.

Stakeholder dialogue is also an instrument to avoid and, possibly, solve conflicts or differences of opinion with stakeholders. The SR core subjects 'Human rights' and 'Consumer issues' give attention to this: for example, in the form of establishing formal procedures for complaints handling. According to ISO 26000, organisations should at least develop appropriate mechanisms to solve conflicts or disputes with stakeholders. Such mechanisms could include conversations and discussions with stakeholders, delivering written information, forums in which stakeholders and the organisation can present their visions and work together towards a satisfactory solution, and mediation or arbitration procedures (ISO 2010: 77).

8.5 **Enhancing credibility**

At the beginning of this book the usage of standards and participation in certification schemes, trademarks and labels were discussed as ways in which organisations can enhance their credibility. In general, external, independent audits strengthen credibility. This will probably be the case for ISO 26000 as well, since it is an ambition of the guideline to become a global, all-encompassing guidance document. Given the authority that the guideline is expected to receive, organisations will likely start to see ISO 26000 as a means of increasing the credibility of their SR initiatives: for instance, by stating that they have used the guideline in determining their SR strategy. Organisations

11 This topic is also covered in Chapter 5.

may also gain credibility by participating in industry or sector initiatives in the realm of SR (for example the chemical industry's Responsible Care initiative or the Humanitarian Technology Fund of the Institute of Electrical and Electronic Engineers (IEEE) Foundation). Connecting to SR networks that require good practice for participation, such as CSR Europe, is another strategy for advanced organisations. However, ISO 26000 emphasises that membership of such groups, bodies or networks is not an indicator of the SR level of an organisation. The benefits therefore should be weighed carefully. Does the cost and commitment contribute to the societal commitments of the organisation or is it largely for reputational reasons? Either way, according to the SR guideline, participation should at least lead to some tangible actions by an organisation aimed at improving its SR performance (ISO 2010: 78-80).

Did you know...

PwC's Sustainability barometer from September 2009 showed that of the Dutch companies that claim to be sustainable businesses offering sustainable products and services, only a small percentage provide insight into the how and what of their SR claims.[12]

In Chapter 5 we discussed how stakeholder engagement can be a way of increasing the credibility of SR claims and reports. Examples included using stakeholder consultation in order to understand which SR impact areas are material for the organisation and the inclusion of stakeholders in a SR panel that advises the organisation or can verify its SR performance. The existence of such engagement also enhances trust and confidence in an organisation and contributes to the credibility of its SR initiative.[13]

ISO 26000 provides several suggestions on how to enhance the credibility of communications about SR claims and SR reports, among which are ensuring that the organisation's performance as reported in its sustainability report is

12 Anders Bekken blog, 'De PricewaterhouseCoopers Duurzaamheidbarometer: Duurzaamheid onderdeel strategie', 13 October 2009; www.stichtingmilieunet.nl/andersbekekenblog/duurzaam/de-pricewaterhouseco opers-duurzaamheidbarometer-duurzaamheid-heeft-een-vaste-positie-veroverd. html, accessed 19 March 2011.

13 ISO 26000 emphasises this once more (ISO 2010: 78): 'There are various ways in which an organisation establishes its credibility. One is stakeholder engagement, which involves dialogue with stakeholders and is an important means of increasing confidence that the interests and intentions of all participants are understood. This dialogue can build trust and enhance credibility. Stakeholder engagement can be a basis for involving stakeholders in the verification of an organisation's claims concerning its performance. The organisation and stakeholders can make arrangements for stakeholders to periodically review or otherwise monitor aspects of an organisation's performance.'

comparable over time, is comparable with the performance of similar organisations (in the same sector), contains explanations on why an organisation does not report on certain seemingly relevant SR topics, uses eco-labels or existing SR assessment criteria, and is verified by an external third party.

8.5.1 Solving conflicts and disputes between an organisation and its stakeholders

Another issue related to enhancing the credibility of SR is how an organisation deals with conflicts and disputes with its stakeholders (see also the SR core subjects 'Human rights' and 'Consumer issues' in Chapter 6). The relevance of this topic for implementation concerns the possibility of the emergence of conflicts or different point of view between different stakeholders or groups of stakeholders as a result of the implementation of SR activities.

According to ISO 26000, an organisation should develop mechanisms to solve conflicts or disputes with stakeholders appropriate for the kind of conflict or dispute as well as for the particular stakeholder involved. Moreover, an organisation is supposed to be transparent with respective stakeholders about the procedures it has in place (ISO 2010: 79-80).

8.6 Monitoring and improving SR activities and performance

Sound SR performance depends, among other things, on the commitment of an organisation, supervision, evaluation and review of the activities that are undertaken, the progress that is made, the achievement of formulated objectives and other aspects of the efforts made by an organisation. Constantly monitoring SR performance is a requirement for continuous improvement regarding SR, provided that the obtained insights result in action. By keeping close track of performance, it can be evaluated whether difficulties will arise or have arisen, what the success factors are to achieve formulated goals, whether the organisation is on the right path to realise its SR ambitions and what adjustments might be necessary to achieve the formulated SR goals (ISO 2010: 80). Obviously, SR is not different from other management areas in this respect.

In this context, the organisation can ask itself the following questions (ISO 2010: 81):

- Were objectives and targets achieved as envisioned?

- Did the strategies and processes suit the objectives?

- What worked and why? What did not work and why?

- Was there enough engagement with the objectives?

- Were the objectives appropriate?

- What could have been done better?

- Are all relevant people involved?

Furthermore, there are countless SR tools available to map SR performance. With a SR scan organisations can, often in a short period of time, get an indication of their SR performance, perhaps with a diagnostic that provides a first list of action points that they can directly put into practice. The outcome of such a mapping process can also provide guidance on setting SR objectives. A disadvantage of such tools is that not all SR impact areas are relevant for all organisations. In line with the idea of an organisation-specific SR profile, the ecological and social footprints of a textile manufacturer will be very different from those of a fast food restaurant. Another disadvantage of a scan is that it can never be complete and does not stimulate organisations to innovate, but rather shoehorns them into a box. ISO 26000 does not intend to work in this way either. Although it lists SR core subjects and issues, this content is intended to inspire organisations and help them to get started. It is explicitly not a checklist nor meant to be used as an instrument to find out to what degree an organisation is 'SR ready'. For these reasons every scan or mapping tool, whether or not based on ISO 26000, should be taken with a certain amount of scepticism and organisations should not place too much importance on such instruments. In Annex 3 of this book, an example of an instrument for a scan is given, which can be used by organisations to map their SR performance. The point of departure of this instrument, however, is that an organisation first decides what its relevant SR impact areas are and decides (or has decided) what its ambition in those specific areas is. Consequently, this document is intended to be used by employees of the organisation that already have significant knowledge of the SR performance in respective areas. Of course, this document can be used periodically and does not only have to serve as an initial scan, but can also be a monitoring instrument.

ISO 26000 again proposes that stakeholders can play an important part in the evaluation of the SR performance of an organisation. For instance, an organisation could, in cooperation with stakeholders, look at whether the SR goals that have been formulated are still realistic or ambitious enough and, furthermore, it can learn from the experiences of stakeholders involved with or affected by SR activities. New opportunities, changes in expectations regarding the organisation and broader developments in society can also be mapped in this way. Moreover, involving stakeholders in this process can contribute to increasing the reliability of the information on which the organisation bases its decisions. Regarding internal stakeholders (management and employees), an organisation can make SR or sustainability criteria part of performance appraisals by assessing the contribution made by different departments in realising the SR objectives of the organisation. The integration of SR criteria in this way shows the SR commitment of the organisation is strong.

Benchmarking against the objectives and achievements of other organisations (for example, SR champions in your industry, competitors or other organisations with which the organisation wants to compare itself) can be useful. Such a process can be useful for past or current activities, but perhaps even more importantly can help to anticipate developments in an industry or sector and evaluate what possible changes and consequences of these changes might mean for the organisation. Examples are changes in laws and regulations that can affect the SR performance of organisations or new opportunities for the organisation with respect to market developments and changing consumer preferences.

Did you know...

29% of FTSE Eurofirst300 listed companies have some commitment to linking remuneration to ESG performance — although concerns exists around the extent to which performance targets are set as 'soft targets' thereby guaranteeing a minimum level of bonus.[14]

Moreover, the SR guideline on 'Monitoring of SR performance' stresses that the use of quantitative objectives and derived performance indicators are not the only considerations. Qualitative aspects of monitoring and softer indicators of SR—and techniques that are suitable to map these—should also be involved in this process.[15]

---

14 Eurosif, 'Remuneration'; www.eurosif.org/research/theme-reports/remuneration, accessed 21 March 2011.
15 'It is also important to recognise that social responsibility is about more than specific achievements in measurable activities, such as reducing pollution and responding to complaints. As social responsibility is based on values, application of principles of social responsibility and attitudes, monitoring may involve more subjective approaches such as interviewing, observing and other techniques for evaluating behaviour and commitments' (ISO 2010: 80).

8.7 **Final words**

To actually make SR a living part of an organisation, a structural approach is necessary. Internal and external buy-in as well as support from top management is essential for this. SR implementation is given a lot of space in ISO 26000 and includes advice on SR communication, enhancing the credibility of SR claims and integrating SR in existing systems and structures. Implementing SR successfully depends on getting the soft side (culture, values, engagement) right, as well as dealing with hard issues (structure, measurement, embedding).

As to which aspects an organisation should give most attention, no general conclusion can be drawn. Furthermore, opinions about this differ from person to person and from organisation to organisation. Perhaps the best advice is that SR should be implemented according to the principle 'and–and'. This means that, despite personal or organisational preferences, a structural approach aimed at creating enthusiasm and support is necessary to truly make SR part of the day-to-day activities of employees and the organisation. In other words, an organisation should invest in relevant SR activities in a structural, deliberate, cooperative and clearly focused manner. Moreover, it should constantly benchmark performance against its stated aims and change these when and if it becomes necessary as developments inside and outside the organisation evolve.

9

Epilogue: final thoughts on (the future of) ISO 26000

9.1 **Introduction**

In this final chapter we give some thought to the future of ISO 26000—for instance, certification and its possible alternatives. Furthermore, to illustrate these reasoning behind the expected and current contractual use of ISO 26000 this will be discussed, despite the fact that the SR guideline clearly states that it is neither meant nor suitable for contractual use. We also look at the potential for changes in the content of ISO 26000. Finally, we reflect on whether the development of ISO 26000 towards a management system is likely or, indeed, desirable.

9.2 **Certification**

One of the most important 'hot topics' and confusions surrounding ISO 26000 is whether organisations will be able to certify against the guideline. As mentioned earlier in this book, the guideline is very clear on this: ISO 26000 is not certifiable and is (in its current form) not suitable for certification either. One of the reasons for this is that working with certification bodies would require organisations to reach some level of compliance with regard to SR. This would be contradictory to the stated aims of the guideline, which is to provide guidance to all organisations in formulating their policies on social responsibility. Certification equals exclusion of those not able to comply. Besides, if we look at the current form and structure of the guideline, it cannot be used for certification. At the same time, it seems apparent that there is a demand from organisations for exactly that. Our research (Brandsma *et al.* 2009) showed that over 63% of respondents believed that certification or some other kind of label would be beneficial for organisations to demonstrate that they work in a socially responsible way. Increasing the recognition and credibility of SR-related work is a key reason for this.

As things stand, there is no certifying institution that is allowed to give out an ISO 26000 certificate resulting from an independent third-party assurance of a SR policy, stating that the company 'meets the requirements' of ISO 26000 or the degree to which an organisation works in line with ISO 26000's advice. There has been a forceful lobby for this by companies in the developed world. Despite the fact that there was no stakeholder group completely against the idea of certification, there were objections from some business organisations because of anticipated high costs. It was finally seen as especially important that the guideline could be linked to other, existing standards; as a result, arguments for a new certificate became less important.

However, the fact that ISO 26000 is not currently certifiable, does not mean that a certifiable alternative will not be developed. It is quite conceivable that the SR guideline will undergo radical changes and, in a different form, may become certifiable. In line with the suggestions made by the guideline itself about increasing the credibility of SR claims, certification of an evolved or 'advanced' version of ISO 26000 could be a means to overcome a number of the obstacles which currently limit its use such as its non-verifiability or difficult wording. An organisation with a SR policy or management system that is 'ISO 26000 certified' would probably need to deal with fewer practical problems regarding the credibility of its SR claims compared to an uncertified competitor. Some, of course, would argue that a key strength of ISO 26000 is that it is *not* certifiable. Organisations must continually show that they are credibly performing SR-related activities in line with core principles. The process does not end once a framed certificate is hanging in reception.

9.2.1 Auditing of ISO 26000

The fact that ISO 26000 is not certifiable does not mean that it is impossible to audit an organisation's SR policy guided by or based on ISO 26000. On the contrary, it is, for instance, possible to perform a conformity assessment, which assesses the degree to which an organisation has used ISO 26000 as a guide to integrate social responsibility into its values and practices. It is to be expected that many organisations and, in particular, consultancies will offer some sort of ISO 26000 audit. In fact, this is already happening. Several consultancies offer ISO 26000 auditing services, in part based on the assumption that, after the audit, they can guide the respective organisation towards a SR policy that incorporates the principles of ISO 26000 in more depth. Several of those consultants have even developed their own bespoke ISO 26000 'certificates' or testimonials. Another recent phenomenon is a SR 'certificate' that is partly, but not entirely, based on ISO 26000. Yet other consultancies give out ISO 26000 awards to the organisations they themselves worked for.[1] Many of these efforts to date could, perhaps, be seen as rather self-serving, self-congratulatory marketing efforts rather than genuine attempts to reward or recognise excellence. In fact, it could be argued that such initiatives are not in line with one of the key SR principles of ISO 26000, namely, 'Ethical behaviour', since certification is explicitly excluded by the guideline. During an international ISO 26000 meeting in Quebec in 2009, it was emphasised that every offer to certify an organisation according to ISO 26000, or any claim to be ISO 26000 certified, is a misinterpretation of the intent and purpose of the guideline. This passage has become part of the guideline (ISO 2010: vii).

Some of the organisations offering services related to ISO 26000 pride themselves on their SR expertise, whether or not this is combined with auditing experience in the field of management system norms. Others are mainly basing their offerings on their experience with the auditing of management system norms and less on their SR expertise. Besides offering auditing services, many consultancies offer services to organisations that want to work in alignment with ISO 26000. An entire industry is growing up around ISO 26000 which, again, illustrates the (expected) authority of the guideline.

---

1 Duurzaam Ondernemen, 'Mondial Movers ontvangt ISO 26000 Koploperbokaal'; www.duurzaam-ondernemen.nl/detail_press.phtml?act_id=9799, accessed 21 March 2011.

9.2.2 Types of auditing

There are likely to be several different types of ISO 26000 audit (e.g, third-party auditing, whereby the audit of the SR policy is performed by an experienced consultancy). Self-auditing against ISO 26000 is also possible although this will reduce the credibility of the audit (as it is not independent). However, it is a relatively easy, cheap and therefore feasible approach, especially for SMEs. The head of SR or another manager responsible for SR within an organisation could do the audit or an audit team could be appointed. Such a team might consist of people not directly involved with SR policy, such as the owner or a board member, a human resources manager, a quality, environment and/or safety manager, a purchasing or logistics manager, or a member of the staff council or trade union. The selection of team members would depend on both the SR profile and the SR priorities of the organisation. Another approach might be to use a peer organisation as an external-party auditor. For example, a police authority might choose a neighbouring force. An organisation might also choose an acknowledged SR leader (whether or not guided by ISO 26000). The experience of such an organisation, especially in the field of SR implementation, can be very valuable. Yet another option for external auditing is second-party auditing whereby a stakeholder that has specific SR aspirations or requirements for the organisation (or has other reasons for an interest in the effective development and implementation of a SR policy), such as a customer, performs the audit. Finally, and probably the approach most in line with the overarching philosophy of ISO 26000, an audit could be performed by a panel of the organisation's most important stakeholders. Trade unions could be particularly important here.

What we can certainly anticipate is that there will be many (online) instruments, tools and scans related to ISO 26000 which will become available in order to help organisations determine, or at least give some indication of, the degree to which they already work according to ISO 26000.[2] An ISO 26000 quick scan can be found in Annex 1.

9.3 **Contractual use**

In this book we have stressed that ISO 26000 is an important and globally recognised guideline for building organisational policies on social responsibility.

---

2 Strictly speaking this is not a form of auditing.

It has three particular strengths: the idea of an organisation-specific SR profile allows for flexibility in how SR is interpreted and implemented depending on the ambitions and activities of the user (philosophy); the elaborate multistakeholder consultation process that was undertaken in the many years of development and the inclusion of this approach as a central pillar the final guideline (legitimacy); and finally the association with the internationally-acknowledged and recognisable ISO label (authority). Therefore, either intentionally or not, the guideline will receive the character of a norm—in the sense that it will bee seen as something an organisation should comply with if it wants its SR efforts to be taken seriously.

Already, several organisations, including some from the public sector, are referring to ISO 26000 in tenders and as a criterion for the (pre)selection of proposals. Partly this stems from ignorance and a general air of confusion about what ISO 26000 can or cannot be used for as it is explicitly stated in the guideline that it is not meant for contractual or legal use. However, it also indicates that ISO 26000 is desired in the marketplace as a powerful, all-encompassing benchmark standard for SR. One can foresee that the desire of ISO for the genie to remain in the bottle marked 'for guidance only' may be frustrated. It is very likely that ISO 26000, or parts thereof, will become increasingly requested for project proposals and eventually may even be used as a critical element of sustainable purchasing by both companies and governments.

9.4 **Future changes in ISO 26000**

After the official publication, every ISO standard is periodically revised. ISO 26000 will not be an exception to this. Such a revision does not necessarily result in very radical changes, but some slight improvements are always made, based on experiences, recent developments and new insights. Neither the general SR principles nor the core subjects and issues are expected to change drastically during the coming years, despite the fact that ISO 26000 states that the social responsibilities of organisations are subject to continuous—and perhaps fast-moving—change. Instead, we may anticipate that the most important changes will probably be found at the level of organisational application, since in that area the changes are the largest as well as the most radical for the specific organisation. So, whenever a organisation changes or broadens its activities, it will have to re-evaluate the significance and the sphere of influence of the SR issues in ISO 26000, but this is obviously not related to

Box 9.1 **The future of ISO 26000: observations from research**

The research conducted by the IISD (Perera 2008) about the materiality of the SR principles and SR core subjects that are included in ISO 26000 concludes that the guideline has the potential to become an extensive guide to increase the adoption of SR among SMEs (see also Interlude II). However, the research also throws up criticisms. One of these is the observation that ISO 26000 is mainly a relevant guideline for companies that are export-oriented, form part of an international supply chain, produce products or services that are related to people and the environment, are financed by ethical investors and run by people that are aware of the urgency of sustainable development. ISO 26000 cannot, therefore, be relevant for many SMEs. In addition, according to the IISD, it is important that the relation between sustainable development and the economic activities of companies should become more evident. In this process, ISO 26000 could play a prominent role, but chooses not to, as became clear in Chapter 2. Finally, just like other SR-related standards such as SA8000 or eco-certification schemes, ISO 26000 can, according to the IISD, play a role in creating a level playing field for fair trade and economic development. At the same time, such standards can be used to raise trade barriers, mainly to the disadvantage of producers in developing countries (though ISO 26000 clearly states that this is not its intention).

Our own 2009 research in the Netherlands (Brandsma *et al.* 2009) indicated that the reception for ISO 26000 is likely to be positive. Despite many uncertainties, 40% of our respondents felt ISO 26000 would offer additional value to their organisations and more than a third were considering applying the guideline to their own SR programmes. At the same time, approximately the same number expected to face obstacles with the scope of the guideline, its voluntarism and customer ambivalence towards it. More than 25% felt that it offered too little guidance and required no concrete commitment.

changes in the guideline. The changes will probably not take place at a global level and therefore have no influence on the contents of the guideline—the last large development that was integrated into the guideline was in fact the agenda-setting of climate change as part of the global (businesses) agenda. So, there is unlikely to be any radical change to the content anytime soon. One reason for this may be the rather generalised content in the final version. Still, new issues are certainly likely to enter or gain increased importance in the SR landscape, and some of the conventions and agreements on which ISO 26000 is partly based will also themselves be revised or amended.

In our opinion, there is room for improvement. In the field of SR implementation (Clause 7): for instance, many organisations may come across bottlenecks. There could also be more attention for the topic of engaging employees with SR. Furthermore, there could be more attention directed towards the development process of SR strategies within organisations, and to how employees can be involved and play an active role in this. Another neglected topic, we feel is societal, social and organisational innovation.

Of the SR core subjects and issues within ISO 26000, 'Organisational governance' stands out as an exception. No SR issues are discussed or specified for this core subject. This seems strange and should also be addressed. For example, there could be attention devoted to topics such as the relationship between supervisory and management boards or the importance of SR criteria in directors' remuneration or the receiving of gifts.

Another probable area for further development is in sector supplements, as is the case for the GRI guidelines for sustainability reporting. Sector supplements would, in the context of ISO 26000, and in addition to the existing SR core subjects and issues, address sector-specific SR themes and could be potentially developed by sector organisations.

Finally, we come to the perennial problem of SMEs. ISO 26000 aims to be useful and applicable to all organisations, but is it really, in its current form? We think that an additional guideline for SMEs is necessary and will come into existence. Such a guideline could include a specification of SR issues for every SR core subject to match the needs and perceptions of SMEs, but also contain real-life examples and tips for SR implementation.

9.5 **Final words**

Will ISO 26000 be developed as a (certifiable) management system in the future after all, complete with requirements instead of suggestions and advice? That is without a doubt plausible, but not in its current form. The fact that ISO 26000 is not suitable for certification purposes does not exclude it from becoming a management system. ISO Guide 72 (ISO 2001) distinguishes three types of management system standards, of which only one can be certified. This means that it is possible to develop an ISO 26000 management system without certification being a requirement. Furthermore, wouldn't a management system standard be useful, especially for SR? Since the core of a management system is the systematic control of the organisation's processes in order to achieve set goals and improve processes, through feedback and, when required, change (improvement), then SR seems a suitable case for treatment. It is expected that many organisations will express a desire for exactly this, since it will help them to add more structure to their SR policies. Of course, many organisations already have experience of working with management systems, and the resistance to working with another may not be great. Much could be retained: the SR profile, for example.

We forecast that the market will speak on this issue. As initiatives related to ISO 26000 increase, and the use of the guideline for contractual purposes grows, the need for a certifiable social management system—an SMS—will become clear.

Bibliography

Axentis and the Open Compliance and Ethics Group (2008) *Survey highlights: Code of conduct survey reveals serious weaknesses* (Scottsdale, AZ: OCEG).

Barnard, C. (1938) *The functions of the executive* (Cambridge, MA: Harvard University Press).

Bowen, H. (1953) *Social responsibilities of the businessman* (New York: Harper & Row).

Brandsma, M., L. Moratis and T. Cochius (2009) *Motivations for and potential barriers of ISO 26000 uptake in the Netherlands* (Rotterdam: CSR Academy)

Business in the Community (2009) *Survey report of consumer attitudes in Ireland towards corporate responsibility* (Dublin: Business in the Community Ireland).

Carroll, A.B. (1979) 'A three-dimensional conceptual model of corporate performance', *Academy of Management Review* 4.4: 497-505.

—— (1999) 'Corporate social responsibility: Evolution of a definitional construct', *Business & Society* 38.3: 268-95.

Centraal Bureau van de Statistiek (2009) *Monitor Duurzaam Nederland 2009* (Den Haag: Centraal Bureau voor de Statistiek).

Chhabara, R. (2009) 'Stakeholder panels: reaching a critical mass', Ethical Corporation, June 2009; www.ethicalcorp.com/content.asp?ContentID=6491h.

Cochius, T., and L. Moratis (2009) *Eindrapportage Strategische Verkenning MVO: Leren van koplopers in binnen- en buitenland* (unpublished research paper).

Crosby, P. (1986) *Quality without tears: The art of hassle free management* (New York: McGraw-Hill International).

Davis, K. (1960) 'Can business afford to ignore social responsibilities?', *California Management Review* 2.3: 70-76.

—— (1973) 'The case for and against business assumption of social responsibilities', *Academy of Management Journal* 16.2: 312-22.

De Lange, W., and J. Koppens (2004) *De duurzame arbeidsorganisatie* (Amsterdam: WEKA).

De Swart, E., L. Moratis, C. Bertens and S. Lap (2010) *Kansen voor open doel* (Assen, Netherlands: Van Gorcum).

Drucker, P.F. (1999) *Management challenges of the 21st century* (New York: Harper Business).

Edelman (2007) *2007 Edelman Trust Barometer* (Chicago: Edelman)

Edwards, T., P. Marginson, P. Edwards, A. Ferner and O. Trensakis (2007) *Corporate social responsibility in multinational companies: Management initiatives or negotiated agreements* (Geneva: ILO).

Eells, R. (1956) *Corporate giving in a free society* (New York: Harper).

Elkington, J. (1997) *Cannibals with forks: The triple bottom-line of 21st century business* (Oxford, UK: Capstone Publishing).

European Stakeholder Forum on CSR (2004) *Report of the Round Table on fostering CSR among SMEs* (Brussels: European Commission).

Friedman, M. (1970) 'The social responsibility of business is to increase it profits', *New York Times Magazine*, 13 September 1970, reprinted in T. Donaldson and P. Werhane, *Ethical Issues in Business: A Philosophical Approach* (Englewood Cliffs, NJ: Prentice Hall, 2nd edn 1983).

Friedman, T. (2005) *The world is flat* (New York: Farrar, Straus & Giroux).

GITP (2008) *Diversiteitsbarometer* (Amsterdam: GITP)

Global Footprint Network (2010) *Ecological footprint atlas 2010* (Oakland, CA: Global Footprint Network)

Goodijk, R. (2006) 'Ondernemen in interactie met de omgeving', in L. Moratis and M. van der Veen (eds.), *Basisboek MVO* (Assen, Netherlands: Van Gorcum).

Googins, B., V. Veleva, C. Pinney, P. Mirvis, R. Carapinha and R. Raffaelli (2009) *State of corporate citizenship in the United States: Weathering the storm* (Boston, MA: Boston Center for Corporate Citizenship).

Handy, C. (1998) *The hungry spirit* (London: Arrow Books).

Heald, M. (1957) 'Management's responsibility to society: The growth of an idea', *Business History Review* 31.4: 375-84.

Hoevenagel, R. (2004) *Maatschappelijk verantwoord ondernemen in het midden- en bedrijf* (Zoetermeer, Netherlands: EIM Business & Policy Research).

—— (2007) *Maatschappelijk verantwoord ondernemen in het grote MKB: Verslag van een internetenquête* (Zoetermeer, Netherlands: EIM Business & Policy Research).

ISO (2001) *Guidelines for the justification and development of management system standards* (Geneva: ISO).

—— (2010) *Guidance on social responsibility* (Geneva: ISO).

Johnson, G., and K. Scholes (1999) *Exploring corporate strategy* (Harlow, UK: Prentice Hall).

Karnani, A. (2010) 'The case against corporate social responsibility', *Wall Street Journal*, 23 August 2010.

Keijzers, G., F. Boons and R. van Daal (2002) *Duurzaam ondernemen: Strategie van bedrijven* (Dordrecht, Netherlands: Kluwer).

Kotler, P., and N. Lee (2005) *Corporate social responsibility: Doing the most good for your company and your cause* (Hoboken, NJ: John Wiley).

Kreps, T. (1940) *Measurement of the social performance of business* (Palo Alto, CA: Stanford University Press).

Leipziger, D. (2003) *The corporate responsibility code book* (Sheffield, UK: Greenleaf Publishing).

Maguire, J.W. (1963) *Business and society* (New York: McGraw-Hill).

Management Team (2006) 'Homo's ontbreken in top bedrijfsleven: Het roze plafond', 23 August 2006; www.mt.nl/1/3307/home/homo-39-s-ontbreken-in-top-bedrijfsleven-het-roze-plafond.html.

McAdam, R., and D. Leonard, (2003) 'Corporate social responsibility in a total quality management context: Opportunities for sustainable growth', *Corporate Governance* 3.4: 36-45

Meadows, D.H., D.L. Meadows, J. Randers and W.W. Behrens III (1972) *The limits to growth: A report for the Club of Rome's project on the predicament of mankind* (New York: Universe Books).

Mihalache, S.S., and F. Stremțan (2010) 'Study regarding the perception of the CSR concept among the Alba Iulia Enterprises', *Annales Universitatis Apulensis Series Oeconomica* 12.2: 766-74.

Mintzberg, H., B. Ahlstrand and J. Lampel (1998) *Strategy safari: A guided tour through the wilds of strategic management* (New York: The Free Press).

OECD (2008) *Guidelines for multinational enterprises* (Paris: OECD).

Peborgh, E. (2008) *Sustainability 2.0: Networking enterprises and citizens to face world challenges* (Buenos Aires: Ernesto van Peborgh).

Perera, O. (2008) *How material is ISO 26000 social responsibility to small and medium-sized enterprises?* (Winnipeg: IISD)

Porter, M., and M. Kramer (2006) 'Strategy and society: The link between competitive advantage and corporate social responsibility', *Harvard Business Review*, December 2006: 78-92.

Prahalad, C.K. (2004) *The fortune at the bottom of the pyramid: Eradicating poverty through profits* (Upper Saddle River: Wharton School).

Smith, A. (1759) *The theory of moral sentiments* (Indianapolis, IN: Liberty Classics, 1976).

—— (1776) *An inquiry into the nature and causes of the wealth of nations* (London: W. Strahan & T. Cadell).

Stern, N. (2006) *Stern review: The economics of climate change* (London: Treasury Office of the Government of the United Kingdom and Northern Ireland).

UNDP (United Nations Development Programme) (2008) *Fighting climate change: Human solidarity in a divided world. Human Development Report 2007–2008* (New York: UNDP).

Van Dijk, J.J.J. (1975) *Vermaatschappelijking van organisaties* (Leiden, Netherlands: Stenfert Kroese).

Van Weele, A.J. (2009) *Purchasing and supply chain management: Analysis, strategy, planning and practice* (Andover, UK: Cengage Learning Business Press).

Visser, W. (2011) *The age of responsibility: CSR 2.0 and the new DNA of business* (London: Wiley).

Volkskrant (2007) *Verantwoord ondernemen Nederlands exportartikel*, 24 April 2007.

Votaw, D. (1972) 'Genius became rare: A comment on the doctrine of social responsibility', *California Management Review* 16.2: 25-31.

Wall, C. (2008) *Buried treasure: Discovering and implementing the value of corporate social responsibility* (Sheffield, UK: Greenleaf Publishing).

Walton, C.C. (1967) *Corporate social responsibilities* (Belmont, CA: Wadsworth Publishing).

WWF (2010) *China ecological footprint report 2010: Biocapacity cities and development* (China: WWF).

Annex 1
ISO 26000 Quick Scan

A1.1 **Introduction to the ISO 26000 Quick Scan**

The ISO 26000 Quick Scan has been developed in order to give you an idea of the contents of the guideline and to enable you to obtain an indication of the extent to which your organisation already works according to ISO 26000.

The scan consists of 14 items that you can go through quickly and simply. Each item needs to be scored from the perspective of your organisation. Every score you attribute is included in the final score at the end of the scan. The scores on all 14 items result in an overall score. By making a simple calculation, it is possible to arrive at a percentage (when you score 100%, your organisation fully works in accordance with ISO 26000). The scan, including calculating the percentage, can be completed in less than 15 minutes.

A1.2 **The Quick Scan**

Please indicate for each of the items below whether or not this is applicable to your organisation. When you have finished the list of items, you are ready to calculate your organisation's ISO 26000 score.

Item 1 (Clauses 5 and 6): Next to our goal to safeguard our organisation's continuity, we pay attention to social and environmental issues.

Your answer	❏ Yes	❏ No	❏ Don't know

Item 2 (Clause 6): We consciously strive towards realising economic value for our organisation by paying attention to social and environmental issues.

Your answer	❏ Yes	❏ No	❏ Don't know

Item 3 (Clauses 4, 5 and 7): We have determined our social responsibilities by analysing our organisation's sustainability impact (our social and environmental footprint/the areas where we create the largest sustainability effects) and act accordingly.

Your answer	❏ Yes	❏ No	❏ Don't know

Item 4 (Clause 7): We have formulated a number of clear SR priorities for our organisation and have identified objectives for these priorities.

Your answer	❏ Yes	❏ No	❏ Don't know

Item 5 (Clause 6): Sustainability considerations are an integral part of the decision-making processes and the planning of activities within our organisation.

Your answer	❏ Yes	❏ No	❏ Don't know

Item 6 (Clauses 4 and 6): Our organisation complies with international norms of behaviour that have been established and agreed upon, such as ILO conventions on child labour and indigenous people, UN Global Compact and the OECD Guidelines for Multinational Enterprises.

Your answer	❏ Yes	❏ No	❏ Don't know

Item 7 (Clauses 4 and 5): We have identified the interests and expectations of our most important stakeholders and make sure that we take them into account when we act.

Your answer	❏ Yes	❏ No	❏ Don't know

Item 8 (Clauses 4 and 5): We are continuously working on engaging stakeholders in our operations, including in the field of SR.

Your answer	❏ Yes	❏ No	❏ Don't know

Item 9 (Clauses 4 and 6): If we can't do business in a fair and honest way, we won't do business at all.

Your answer	❏ Yes	❏ No	❏ Don't know

Item 10 (Clause 6): We invest in community involvement activities, such as the sponsoring of cultural events and the development of the local communities that we operate in, and we encourage employee volunteering.

Your answer	❑ Yes	❑ No	❑ Don't know

Item 11 (Clauses 5 and 7): We are continuously working to create awareness and support among management and employees for our SR efforts and try to actively engage them in these efforts.

Your answer	❑ Yes	❑ No	❑ Don't know

Item 12 (Clause 7): Our SR efforts already have existing systems, procedures and structures within our organisation.

Your answer	❑ Yes	❑ No	❑ Don't know

Item 13 (Clause 7): We monitor the extent to which we realise our SR objectives and improve our SR performance every year.

Your answer	❑ Yes	❑ No	❑ Don't know

Item 14 (Clauses 4, 5 and 7): We offer a balanced insight into our SR performance by communicating it to our stakeholders (e.g. by producing a sustainability report).

Your answer	❑ Yes	❑ No	❑ Don't know

A1.3 **Your score**

Almost every item in this ISO 26000 Quick Scan relates to multiple aspects and sections of ISO 26000. The four most important clauses of the guideline (Clauses 4, 5, 6 and 7) have a central role in the scan. The items have been formulated in a way that you have six scores on each of these clauses.

The answer 'Yes' corresponds with 1 point, while both the answers 'No' and 'Don't know' correspond with 0 points. Use the table below to calculate your score.

Item	Answer	Points	Clause 4	Clause 5	Clause 6	Clause 7
1						
2						
3						
4						
5						
6						
7						
8						
9						
10						
11						
12						
13						
14						
A	Points per clause					
B	Score under A divided by 6 then × 100		%	%	%	%
			Score Clause 4	Score Clause 5	Score Clause 6	Score Clause 7
D	Average score Clause 4 and 6		%			← Score for the 'contents of SR'
E	Average score Clause 5 and 7		%			← Score for the 'process of SR'
F	Average score D + E		%			← Final score ISO 26000 Quick Scan

A1.4 **Scores on the four central clauses in ISO 26000**

This Quick Scan is based on the four central clauses in ISO 26000 (4–7).

Clause 4 specifies the principles of SR, such as transparency, respect for stakeholder interests and ethical behaviour.

Your score: ____%

Clause 5 is about mapping stakeholders, their interests and expectations, and creating stakeholder engagement.

Your score: ____%

Clause 6 identifies the SR core subjects and issues, such as organisational governance, the environment and consumer issues.

Your score: ____%

Clause 7 offers guidelines and suggestions for the integration of SR throughout organisations and elaborates, among other things, on aligning SR with existing structures, systems and procedures, measuring and improving SR and communicating about SR performance.

Your score: ____%

A1.4.1 Score on the 'contents of SR'

Clause 4 (principles of SR) and Clause 6 (SR core subjects and issues) together comprise the **contents of your organisation's SR policy**, or the SR subject matter. This relates to whether or not your organisation takes the ISO 26000 SR principles as a foundation, applies these in practice, and the extent to which your organisation recognises the core subjects and issues.

Your score: ____%

A1.4.2 Score on the 'process of SR'

Clause 5 (stakeholder engagement) and Clause 7 (guidelines for SR integration) together comprise the **process of your organisation's SR policy**, or the implementation of SR. This relates to whether or not you apply the guidelines that ISO 26000 offers to successfully implement SR in your organisation.

Your score: ____%

Annex 2
An exercise to identify stakeholders' interests and expectations

A2.1 Background information on stakeholder identification

Respecting stakeholder interests is one of the general principles in ISO 26000. In order to do this, organisations need to be capable of identifying their stakeholders and the interests they have, in order to create stakeholder engagement (see Chapter 5 for further background information on stakeholder identification).

A2.2 An exercise for mapping stakeholders' interests

The exercise below is a way of identifying stakeholders and of mapping their interests and expectations in the context of an organisation's social responsibilities. This exercise can be done by an individual, but we suggest undertaking it with a group, since this will contribute to the richness of information. We also suggest that this exercise should be used both for identifying the interests of the stakeholders and their expectations towards the SR performance of an organisation.

1. Write the names of every stakeholder that you can think for your organisation on a post-it note. Put these post-it notes on a large table, a whiteboard, a flip-chart or on a wall.

2. When all possible stakeholders have been identified, write down the primary interests of the different stakeholders on new post-it notes of a different colour.

3. Do the same (again in a different colour) for the expectations of the stakeholders towards the organisation's SR performance.

4. Start grouping the interests and expectations (identical or similar interests and expectations should be categorised in the same group). Now place together the post-it notes to show each stakeholder with the applicable interests and expectations. When a stakeholder fits with more than one group of interests and expectations, make an extra post-it note showing the stakeholder's name and place this with other applicable group(s).

5. Make a page (A4 format) for each stakeholder with the post-it note showing the name of the stakeholder and the various notes with interests and expectations that correspond to this stakeholder. Also write down your organisation's name on an A4-sized page.

6. Place the A4-sized page with your organisation's name on it in the middle of the table, flip-chart or wall. Place the other A4-sized pages showing the stakeholders and their interests and expectations around this page (in a star-shaped form, for instance). Determine the importance of the various stakeholders. The more important a stakeholder is, the closer it should be to the central page showing the name of the organisation in the middle.

A typical result is depicted below.

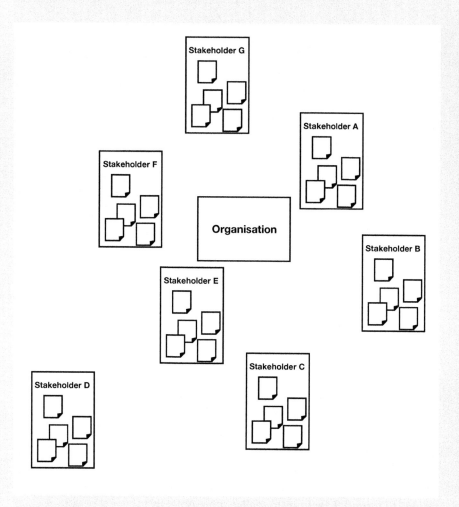

7. Based on this ordering, determine what type of relationship the organisation should develop with the respective stakeholders, the intensity of this relationship, and the instruments that the organisation could deploy to communicate and engage with this stakeholder.

Annex 3
The SR performance form

A4.1 **About the SR performance form**

Every organisation can quickly and simply determine its current SR performance with the SR performance form. In order to do so, the organisation should take its SR priorities or focus areas as a starting point and specify these as completely as possible, including relevant sub-categories. One way of doing this is by using the impact/influence matrix that was introduced in Chapter 7 (Figure 7.1, page 154). The SR performance form also provides an opportunity for the organisation to discover to what extent actual performance is in line with the organisation's ambitions? The SR performance form also asks for the setting of short-, medium- and long-term objectives, and challenges organisations to formulate actions to realise these objectives.

The focus areas and the sub-areas that can be included in the forms do not necessarily have to correspond with core subjects and issues as set out in ISO 26000.

A4.2 **Who should complete the form?**

The SR performance form can be completed in several different ways:

- By a SR working group during a meeting
- By individual members of a SR working group prior to a meeting

- By distributing the forms among employees that have the information needed or who have a strong opinion about the SR performance of the organisation

- By, or in cooperation with, external stakeholders

It is recommended that users should always formulate the actions needed as practically and completely as possible, and make clear choices in answering the different questions. It is also recommended to have different people within the organisation complete the same forms in order to obtain a detailed insight into the organisation's SR performance and to properly identify the correct actions to realise the objectives. If employees or stakeholders are asked to complete the forms, it is also useful to compare the findings to those of a SR working group. In doing so, performance gaps can be identified.

A4.3 **The form**

Focus area:	[Enter your SR priorities and possible sub-priorities]
Sub-area:	

A. Performance

Question: How does our organisation currently perform in this area?

B. Ambition

Question: To what extent is the current performance acceptable in the light of the ambitions of our organisation?

Totally unacceptable ← 1   2   3   4   5   6   7   8   9   10 → Totally acceptable

C. Existing policies

Question: Do policies aimed at improving this performance currently exist in our organisation?

❏ Yes   ❏ No   ❏ Don't know

D. Objectives

Question: What level of performance should our organisation aim for?

Performance level in 1 year	
Performance level in 3 to 5 years	

E. Actions

Question: What actions should be taken in order to realise the aspired performance levels?

Actions to realise performance level aimed at in 1 year	
Actions to realise performance level aimed at in 3–5 years	

Annex 4
Millennium Development Goals

A4.1 Background to the Millennium Development Goals

The UN Millennium Development Goals (MDGs), a set of sustainability goals that ISO 26000 refers to, are aimed at eradicating poverty and spurring development by improving social and economic conditions in the world's poorest countries. In September 2000, leaders of 189 countries signed the UN Millennium Declaration which committed them to achieving the MDGs. Currently, 192 UN member states and at least 23 international organisations are active in pursuing the MDGs. The MDGs have been translated into eight concrete goals that should be realised by 2015. For each of these goals performance indicators have been formulated in order to measure progress.

One of the main criticisms of the MDGs is that they are too ambitious. By now, it is clear that these goals will not be realised in those key parts of the world where they were intended to have the greatest impact, such as in many African countries. According to various experts and studies, such as a study funded by the Bill and Melinda Gates Foundation into maternal mortality rate, the target date of 2015 is unattainable. In 2010, UN Secretary-General Ban Ki-moon said the MDGs are still attainable should world leaders exercise political leadership.

Many countries have crafted agreements between government, businesses and NGOs aimed at sustainable development that include aspirations towards achieving the MDGs. In the Netherlands, for instance, Dutch cities can participate in a nationally coordinated campaign and can earn the label 'Millennium City' by contributing to achieving the MDGs in various ways.[1]

A4.2 **The eight MDGs**

The MDGs include the following goals:

- End poverty and hunger
- Universal education
- Gender equality
- Child health
- Maternal health
- Combat HIV/AIDS
- Environmental sustainability
- Global partnership

1 For more information, www.un.org/millenniumgoals.

Annex 5
The Global Compact

A5.1 **Background to the Global Compact**

Many international organisations have developed some sort of SR initiative, guideline or code of conduct, either of a sector-specific nature or of general applicability. One of the most prominent of the latter category, and one that has been adopted by nearly 9,000 companies from over 130 countries, is the UN Global Compact.[1] This was established in 2000 by the then UN Secretary-General Kofi Annan in order to connect business, UN organisations, labour unions and NGOs with the purpose of making progress on ten themes in the field of human rights, labour conditions, environmental protection and corruption

The aim of the Global Compact is to integrate these ten important principles in the activities of global business and, by doing so, encourage structural action to further UN goals, including the Millennium Development Goals. By combining the forces and strengths of all parties involved, the Global Compact aims to promote the cause of socially responsible business, so helping business to make a contribution to counter the negative effects of globalisation.

The Global Compact invites companies to commit to UN and other globally recognised goals, and offers tools and instruments to enable this. It now claims to be the world's largest corporate citizenship and sustainability initiative. Since its inception in 2000, the initiative has grown to more than 8,500 participants, including over 6,000 businesses in 130 countries around the world. Signing the Global Compact means that a company's board commits

1 www.unglobalcompact.org

itself to integrating the ten principles into its operations and annually reports about the progress it has made. If signatories fail to comply with the reporting requirement, they can be delisted. Since 2008, more than 2,000 companies have been expelled from the Global Compact for failing to report.

A5.2 **The Global Compact principles**

The principles of the Global Compact comprise four areas:

- Human rights
- Labour
- Environment
- Anti-corruption

A5.2.1 **Human rights**

The first two principles of the Global Compact have been derived directly from the Universal Declaration of Human Rights:[2]

- Businesses should support and respect the protection of internationally proclaimed human rights
- Businesses should make sure they are not complicit in human rights abuses.

A5.2.2 **Labour**

The next four principles are derived from the 1998 ILO Declaration on Fundamental Principles and Rights at Work:[3]

- Businesses should uphold freedom of association and the effective recognition of the right to collective bargaining
- The elimination of all forms of forced and compulsory labour
- The effective abolition of child labour
- The elimination of discrimination in respect of employment and occupation

---

2 www.un.org/en/documents/udhr/index.shtml
3 www.ilo.org/declaration/thedeclaration/textdeclaration/lang--en/index.htm

A5.2.3 Environment

The next three principles have been derived from the Rio Declaration on Environment and Development:[4]

- Businesses should support a precautionary approach to environmental challenges

- Undertake initiatives to promote greater environmental responsibility

- Encourage the development and diffusion of environmentally friendly technologies

A5.2.4 Anti-corruption

The final principle has been derived from the UN Convention against Corruption:[5]

- Businesses should work against corruption in all its forms, including extortion and bribery

A5.3 The Global Compact and ISO 26000

Interestingly, there has been some tension between the Global Compact and ISO 26000.[6] Georg Kell, Executive Director of the UN Global Compact Office, sent a letter to Robert Steele, ISO's Secretary-General, in June 2009, which expressed his disappointment that ISO 26000 did not give the Global Compact the prominence the UN felt it deserved. The letter asked ISO to remove reference to the Global Compact from the annex of the guideline. Later in 2009, Kell denied that this request indicated disapproval of ISO 26000. The Global Compact, he said, has supported and continues to support ISO in the development of ISO 26000, seeing the two approaches as complementary.

---

4 www.unep.org/Documents.Multilingual/Default.asp?DocumentID=78&ArticleID =1163&l=en
5 www.unodc.org/unodc/en/treaties/CAC/index.html
6 UN Global Compact, 'Global Compact and ISO Clarify Positions, Stress Complementarity', 17 July 2009; www.unglobalcompact.org/NewsAndEvents/news_ archives/2009_07_17.html, accessed 21 March 2011.

About the authors

Lars Moratis is the former director of a specialised CSR consultancy in the Netherlands. He has extensive experience in consulting with companies, governments and NGOs on CSR strategy development and implementation. Currently, he is affiliated with MVO Nederland, the Dutch CSR knowledge centre and is a lecturer/coordinator in a post-graduate CSR programme at the Open University in the Netherlands. He has published three books, including the primary Dutch study book on CSR, and various articles on CSR, ISO 26000 and the interface between CSR and management education.

Timo Cochius is a CSR consultant with BECO, an internationally operating consultancy in sustainable development based in Rotterdam, the Netherlands. He has an academic background in international business administration and is an expert on CSR strategy development, implementation and sustainability reporting. He has extensive experience with consulting with companies, governments and NGOs on different aspects of CSR and ISO 26000 and has published several articles on ISO 26000.